Emotional Abundance:
Become Empowered

Emotional Abundance: Become Empowered

Michelle Bersell

Published by:
Living Source, LLC
740 N. Plankinton, # 310
Milwaukee, WI 53203
www.EmotionalAbundance.com

Copyright © 2007 Michelle Bersell
Interior text design by Tom Davis
ISBN: 978-0-980141-30-6
Library of Congress Control Number: 2007909239

Emotional Abundance: Become Empowered.

First Edition
Printed and bound in the United States of America by Morris Publishing • www.morrispublishing.com • 800-650-7888
1 2 3 4 5 6 7 8 9 10

Acknowledgements

With tears filled with gratitude, I thank my Creator for entrusting me with the wisdom and messages offered in this book. I thank the Divine for all the internal guidance that I received, the words that were given, and the passion to put my energy toward fulfilling my desires. I thank you, God, for all the experiences I have had that have led me to have this intimate and abundant connection with you, leading me ultimately to the truth, power, and abundance within myself. I also give thanks to all the spiritual energies that have guided me throughout this process with love, care, and compassion.

There are also many spirits in the human form that I must give thanks to, beginning with my husband. Thank you, Steve, for being my rock, as well as my supporter both emotionally and physically. With deep and sincere gratitude, I thank you for your deep love and beautiful spirit blessing my life.

I give thanks to my many teachers, especially my Mom, for being willing to go through this journey with me to support me to learn the lessons that make me who I am today. I also want to thank my Dad for the way in which you always show you care and for teaching me the gift of sharing love openly. I have been blessed to have parents who love so much!

To Dr. Darrel Nicks, I give thanks for sharing with me the gift to each of our emotions and how to honor all of our emotions exactly as they are. I would also like to thank my shaman and teacher Shenoa Robinson for teaching me how to begin realigning myself with the truth my spirit speaks.

Immense thanks goes to the teachings, love, and support I have received through my life coaching experience with Faith Namaste. Thank you, Faith, for supporting me to through my journey with greater ease of mind and with wisdom. To my best friend, Dr. Donna Gilman, thank you for being my soul sister. Without your love, wisdom, and compassion, I do not know how I would manage going through life!

With immense love, I thank my children Avery, Jonah, and Eli. You are the most beautiful souls and the greatest teachers in my life. Thank you for being willing to go on this journey with me.

To friends, I thank you for your encouragement and support. To all those who support me in all areas of my life, thank you for helping free my energy in order that I have been able to create this book.

With gratitude and love,

Michelle

Contents

Introduction

What does it mean to live life authentically? Living authentically means we have the freedom to be ourselves and live in a way that feels good and right to us. Yet so many of us struggle with being able to live life abundantly in the manner in which all our physical, emotional, and spiritual needs are met.

As a life coach and psychotherapist, I was embarrassed that I still struggled to live my life as I wanted. I wanted to be filled with purpose, passion, and a joy for living. What I found myself challenged with over and over was my emotions. Even after all the training I received through my psychology program and the therapy I had gone through, at times I could not get a grip on my emotions. I then turned to life coaching to support me to live life more fully. Life coaching provided me with wisdom that supported me to create changes. Through my life coaching, I learned about the Law of Attraction, years before *The Secret* was written. I found even though I was able to dramatically change my thoughts, when strong emotions emerged, I could not control them.

I came to despise my emotions. I hated my "negative" feelings such as sadness, anxiety, or anger. "Why was I feeling this way?" I would ask myself over and over. "My life is not bad. What is wrong with me?" Book after book I read told me it had to do with my thoughts. Trying to control my thoughts just brought me more anguish. I felt even more like a failure that my thoughts could not alleviate the emotional pain I was feeling.

I would have cycles of this pain for months and months. Most of the time I felt pretty good, but when the pain hit, it hit me hard. Eventually I was guided to do something different rather than try to keep buying into strategies that apparently did not work for me. Through my meditations, I was guided to write.

I thought my writing was just going to be me journaling about how I was feeling. My goal was to get these "negative" feelings out of me. I so desperately wanted to be rid of them once and for all. After all, they made me feel like such a failure and a loser.

What I found when I started writing was that I was being guided to finally come to an understanding regarding the purpose of all of our emotions. From a spiritual perspective, there is purpose to how we feel. Once we stop fighting our feelings, we will recognize the gift. Low and behold, **finally I received support that worked!** Even more surprising was that this guidance was coming through to me as I wrote.

The wisdom that is presented throughout this book is nothing that I could have come up with on my own through the training I received as a psychotherapist or a life coach. The training I received, however, did allow me to integrate psychology and Universal Laws to be able to recognize how to apply this latest guidance. My personal experiences, along with those of my clients, have also allowed me to demonstrate how easily we can become blocked through our own internal processes.

The truth is that most of us do not know at all how to address our emotions in a manner that is supportive to us. We have learned how to avoid or ignore our feelings very well. We have also seen modeled those who like to be overly dramatic with their emotions. Neither of those options works well for us.

Finally there is guidance as to how we can work with our feelings, fears and egos in order that we feel at peace, centered, and free to be ourselves. This freedom allows us to manifest all of our heart's desires if we open ourselves to this process. The information provided in this book is not about a quick fix. It is about creating your personal journey, which will enable you to change long-held patterns of trying to cope with your feelings, fears, and ego and to learn how to work with your feelings.

Emotional Abundance: Become Empowered is unique in that it offers readers a process and not a list of tips to mindlessly follow. This book is set up to allow you to have an authentic journey with your emotional self. We begin with simply being able to recognize how we are limiting ourselves and then gradually become more and more aware of our unconscious blocks. Just by becoming more aware, you will see your life change. Add to your consciousness an understanding of each of your most prevalent feelings, fears and ego, and you will now be empowered to live the life that you are intended to live.

We must keep in mind that when it comes to our emotion and sense of empowerment, there is no quick fix. Yet, if you are open to going through this process and allowing your feelings to evolve, you will find an authentic path to claiming your own sense of worth and power. Once you do, the abundance you desire emotionally, spiritually, and materially are yours to enjoy. My hope is that we all learn to fully enjoy the abundance that surrounds us with courage from within our hearts.

Chapter 1
Discover Your Truth

As a psychotherapist and life coach, one of the most common phrases I hear is "I have a good life but... ." Clients share this with me because the majority of them feel blessed to have the careers, family, or lifestyle that they have. However, they also recognize that there is a component, of their life that feels missing or blocked. They know within themselves that without this component they are inhibited from fully living as they would desire. When they come to me, it means they are finally able to admit it out loud and take action to make changes in their life.

Most of us have been inhibited from making changes that support us to truly live because we haven't known the best direction to take. We have been playing the game of life without an owner's manual. Furthermore, some of the rules that have been put forth as to how we should live our life do not work or are not always in our best interest. This can leave us feeling depleted and confused. We end up settling for living a life without passion, awareness, or true understanding of our purpose.

Imagine playing a game without a sense of passion or a full understanding of the rules. Imagine playing without being truly conscious about your actions. Will playing this way achieve the outcome you desire? Will you consistently do well in the game or will you struggle? We all recognize that playing a game in this manner will not support us to consistently have the outcome that we desire.

Now imagine playing a game in which you understand the purpose of why the game works as it does. Imagine being given the tools that support you to play optimally. With the purpose of how the game functions and the proper tools to help you navigate the game with a sense of empowerment, you start to feel good about playing. The better you feel, the more passionate you become toward playing.

We are meant to play in life. What I mean by "play" is putting out in the world our unique, creative selves that are expressed through our passions. In life, we are intended to create by being a full expression of ourselves, for this is how we feel fulfilled. Otherwise, we will feel like there is something missing in our lives. What is truly missing is all of you playing in the game.

Now imagine life in which you are filled with passion. Imagine what life would be like when you understand that our feelings, fears, and even our ego (our false self) are present to support us living our best life. From my own experience, I have shown those whom I have worked with how to consciously and authentically live. Living authentically enables us to experience joy, gratitude, abundance, purpose, and creativity all flowing into our lives with ease. This is how we are supposed to live.

Are you truly playing in life? Are you fully engaged in creating your ideal life or are you half in while another part of you is checked out? Are you playing at all or just on the sidelines observing everyone else?

Most of us are all over the board (pun intended) when we play in life. In a few instances, maybe we felt we were fully engaged in living. We also likely had times in our lives when we stopped playing because life seemed too difficult and challenging. Most of the time, the majority of people are less than halfway in while the other part of them attends to what they call their life. It is not that we intend to live this way. It just seems to happen. We become busy, even overwhelmed at times with the responsibilities, commitments, and worries of our lives. We are caught under a to-do list, whether imaginary or real, that sucks away all our energy. Obviously, with all our energy going toward all these aspects of our lives, we have little time to focus on creating the life we desire.

Choose to Improve Your Game by Playing Differently

Just as with a game, in life there are master players. Master players go through life with ease because they know and trust themselves. For them, life goes the way they intend because they are aligned with the Universal flow of energy and tap into it. Through being tapped into this energy, they feel motivated, inspired, joyful, and grateful to be playing and creating their lives.

To play as a master, you must have a willingness to go beyond what most people do in order to gain insight that shatters typical perceptions. You also must be willing to make a lot of mistakes in order to learn from them and spot them easily the next time they appear. From your efforts, skills become ingrained and naturally flow. You then continue to work to refine your skills that enable you to have this ease and peace toward living.

We are all meant to live life in this manner. Now, more than ever, so much is being revealed to support us to live life with greater ease. We now know that our thinking impacts our reality. Through the Law of Attraction, we understand that we support ourselves better when our thoughts are aligned with our desires. Because our thoughts are creative energy, this is an integral aspect of being able to create our ideal.

Now through this book, it is time to understand another crucial component. This component is our emotions. Our emotions are the key to us being able to create our ideal, because our emotions give us direction. Without this direction, we feel lost, stuck, or limited. For this reason, positive thinking only gets us so far.

Think for a moment how we are able to use positive thinking to get a great parking spot, yet when it comes to manifesting in an area of our life that has meaning to us, such as finding our soul-mate or our dream job, we still struggle. The difference between the two examples is that there is a much greater emotional attachment with trying to find our soul-mate or dream career than in finding a parking spot. If our emotions are not in alignment with the thought we desire to have, our emotions will continue to overpower us. When we struggle, it is because we are not listening to the internal guidance that our emotions are offering us. Therefore, learning *how* to understand and utilize our emotions is integral in order to continue to create the life we desire to live.

How We Currently Understand Our Emotions Does *Not* Support Us

The vast majority of us go about living life emotionally challenged because we do not fully understand our emotional selves. By emotional selves, I mean all aspects of our emotions, including our feelings, fears, and ego. If there is an aspect of our emotional selves that we do not like or does not feel good, we try to deny or ignore its existence. Yet, does this really work? No! In fact, we continue to create struggle and unnecessary difficulty due to this misunderstanding.

What we must take in is that every time we push down our feelings, we are throwing away the golden key to help us create the life we desire. Through our emotions, we are being given the exact direction we need to create what we want. We simply need to be willing and know how to listen. Most of the time, we do not listen, which makes us feel downtrodden by life. When we do not listen, we are working against ourselves. We choose to fight our emotions rather than acknowledge our true sense of how we feel.

In our efforts to try to "think positive," we have inaccurately accessed that it is our duty not only to change our thoughts but also to fight the way we feel. The problem is that all this fighting is tiring! Are we tired of fighting yet? Can we not see the impact that our internal fighting has on the mass consciousness?

The cruelty begins with our treatment toward ourselves and expands into the world. The proof is not only in how much mental health issues have increased over the past few decades but also as we continue to witness violence becoming more and more prevalent. If we want this violence to stop, it must begin with ceasing the inner cruelty. We are cruel to ourselves when we cannot allow ourselves to feel what we feel without causing further pain to ourselves due to our judgments.

We have searched for support to end our cruelty and have been guided over and over to "think positive" and "push past our fears." What we do not realize is that when we are being told these ways to "better" ourselves, we are getting served the same message, which is who we are is not enough. We feel we should be better, different, or more enlightened and therefore we again do not measure up to this self-imposed standard that no human can attain. If our feelings and fears are wrong, that suggests our essence is somehow amiss, because our emotions are an authentic expression of ourselves.

Let me be clear that I feel there is a place for thinking positively. We can change the lens through which we perceive the world in a manner that can be supportive to us. What is happening, however, is that we took this message to heart. We heard that we should no longer have messages within us that are "negative," and so we try to wipe them out of our minds. In doing so, we push ourselves away from our truth. As humans, we are meant to have the full spectrum of feelings we are given.

The other day I was with a woman who demonstrated so clearly that our intentions can be to live a better life yet we find ourselves struggling. This woman felt challenged lately because she was feeling anxious. She shared with me the following: "I know I am not supposed to feel anxious, and so I am trying to think positive. I am trying to see all the good that surrounds me even though I feel like I have a lot going on with my life right now." This woman wants to live her best life, yet she is fighting how she really feels. Her reaction is based on the numerous messages she has received from well-intentioned books, magazines, and people that tell her to push away what is really going on within herself. As this woman does this, she does not feel good because she is fighting her authentic self.

Imagine how you would feel if you did not have to battle yourself anymore and fight against your feelings, fears, and thoughts. Envision the peace within you. All the energy that has gone toward trying to cover up and hide the truth of who you are in each moment is now freed. Can you sense that freedom? I will share with you that it is magic. Once we experience the freedom of ourselves living from our truth, our life will feel magical; because we will have the energy to put toward creating our ideal. We are now able to create our ideal because we are no longer using all our energy trying to push away our truth.

Our emotions are our truth. Our emotions define us, and we kid ourselves if we do not believe this. We can try to hide our truth to others, yet we always have to face our inner knowing of ourselves at the end of the day. Trust me, I have tried to hide the fact that I felt lonely, empty, sad, and frustrated with life. I was able to put on a great mask that made others believe I was confident and self-assured. Yet when I allowed my emotions to surface, I was always confronted with my truth.

My Life as a Master of Disguise
Instead of becoming a master of life, I was a master of disguising how I truly felt inside. On the inside, I felt that there was something innately wrong with me, as I constantly

questioned if I was a good person or good enough in the view of others. In order to feel acceptable to others, I tried to make myself as perfect as possible in every realm of my life. I felt that I had to be physically fit, pretty, well-dressed, charming, humorous, and successful and have a beautifully kept home. Just listing all the areas I was trying to attend to exhausts me. With those standards, no wonder I never felt good enough, as I was setting myself up to fail.

Throughout my journey of disguising my truth, I behaved in ways in which I knew I was going against myself. I had moments in which trying to uphold or deal with the pressure of being someone other than myself took its toll. In those moments, I have lied, cheated, barely ate or gorged myself, and drank and shopped excessively. I was either making those choices to protect my image or to cope with what I could not handle feeling inside. When I made those bad choices, I was internally reiterating to myself what a bad person I truly was. When I felt how bad a person I was, I would try to improve myself only to find that nothing I did felt good enough. I would then turn to coping again. This created a vicious cycle in which I would engage in behaviors that were not in my best interest.

What is interesting is that none of my actions was considered out of the ordinary. Even when I did excessively drink throughout college, where at times I would get sick and even black out, it was not enough that anyone suspected that I was struggling. Unfortunately, there were enough people around me making the same types of choices that my behavior did not signify that anything was wrong. Instead we all seemed to rationalize our bad choices. It appeared most everyone at times seemed to tell a white lie or even a real big one, cheated once or twice on a test they did not study for, eat poorly and then go on a restrictive diet, and did some shopping or drinking therapy to forget about their stresses. The truth was that I did not have an addictive problem such as alcoholism, drug abuse, or an eating disorder. My pain was more subtle and masterly disguised behind the image of somebody I was not.

As I look back on this time in my life, which encompassed my adolescence through my twenties, I realize at least half of my life was spent pretending to be, feel, or act like someone I was not. Even though I went to church every week, did well in school, and liked my family, it did not mean that I was not struggling internally. Yet because nothing appeared to be wrong on the outside, others bought into the notion that I was okay on the inside.

My truth was that when I was by myself, I felt very alone. Even though I projected confidence, I was terribly insecure, as I often questioned my every interaction. My life was centered on me worrying about what others thought of me. My fear was that people would see all these terrible aspects of myself because that was what I was trying to hide. I hid under a guise that was so convincing that no one, not even myself, was aware of the depths of the internal pain I had pushed down within me for so long.

Like a volcano, the pressure underneath eventually became too much, and my pain began to ooze out of me. It first oozed from me as I unexplainably started gaining weight my senior year of college. The weight gain created a crack in my image and my sense of worth sank, as others found me less attractive. Then after college, my pain oozed out more as I struggled finding the dream job I felt certain I would obtain. By this time, my sense of self felt more and more meaningless. The first real eruption was finally triggered by a failed engagement. I felt so ashamed because in my head I blamed myself for not being good enough for someone to want to marry me.

A few years later, another eruption occurred during my doctoral program in clinical psychology in which I was chosen as a group leader. Although this was considered an accomplishment, I felt completely lost. Through being called to lead, I realized I no longer knew what my voice was. I knew the voice of my professor, my mother, my friends, and my husband yet my own was unrecognizable to me at that point.

Both of my eruptions altered me in a way that allowed my pain to flow out of me more and more until I unearthed a piece of myself that had been buried for a long time. It turns out that underneath the pain and drama, there was a gift each time. The gift was discovering my truth in which I finally learned to enjoy and honor myself for who I am authentically.

Discovering My Spiritual Truth

At the same time that my internal truth began to slowly be revealed, I was reawakening to find my spiritual truth as well. When I first began to erupt internally, I was brought down to my knees begging for guidance and support. My first eruption changed my relationship with God because I was pissed. Yes, I got very angry at God! Growing up Catholic, this is not something that I was supposed to do, as I felt I could be somehow punished for doing so. Yet there was no hiding how I felt at that moment when my dream of becoming married was taken away from me. I was a devout person going to church each week, even every holy day, and always saying my prayers. I was doing my best and I was faithful, so why did my dream come crashing down underneath me, I wondered. I felt forgotten and abandoned.

What I found through expressing myself wholeheartedly was that I actually felt closer to my Creator than ever before. God did not punish me for being mad, as I feared. Rather, I felt held, supported, comforted, and guided along my journey. Through the experience of "getting real" with God, I began to realize that the notions that I had been taught about my Creator were inaccurate. I felt more than ever before that I had a personal, loving relationship with my Source. Nevertheless, I still carried many fears about God due to my religious upbringing.

Years later when the next eruption occurred, I was again guided to face both my personal and spiritual truth. With this eruption, I became vulnerable with myself as I allowed myself to express feelings that I never dared to say out loud before. At the same time, I felt the urge to do the same in regard to my perceptions and projections of God. Even though I was raised Christian, deep down there was a part of me that questioned aspects of what I had been taught. Again, I was too afraid to ever admit these out loud. Through my own personal process, I learned how healing it is to share what is locked away deep inside. Due to this positive experience, I finally began to openly admit that some of the beliefs I had did not coincide with what I had been taught. Rather than continue to buy into what I had been told about God, I began questioning my perceptions. This took me on a journey in which I went inward to find what felt true and right to me regarding my Source.

As my internal truth was revealed to me, so was my spiritual truth. My spiritual truth could no longer buy into fearing our Creator or believing God was vengeful. It no longer fit. Although I was at first scared to challenge these notions of what I had been taught, I found myself creating for the first time a real, intimate connection with my Source.

Through my journey, I went from being a highly religious person to becoming a highly spiritual person. My journey expanded from my notion of God being a dominant male figure judging me to knowing a loving Source found in all. From my heart, I recognized the loving message behind the essence of every religion as well as those found in nature and our human Spirit. Because of this shift within me, my notion of the highest essence of our human Spirit is expressed in many different ways such as God, Creator, Source, the Divine, and the Universe. This expansive sense of what I consider the loving essence from which we are all One is what I mean when I interchangeably utilize those words as descriptors.

Nevertheless, my religious upbringing is still a part of me. I found no need to throw out the baby with the bathwater so to speak, as I recognize that there are many truths still to be found in the essence of religious teachings. Because my background is Christianity and those are the teachings that I know most about, I share some of those messages as they pertain to support us to live our best life. In doing so, please know that I have the utmost respect for what feels right for each person to believe.

Discovering the Truth

Having grown as a person both spiritually and emotionally, I felt more at peace with myself and the world. Nevertheless, my emotions would still grab a hold of me in a way that would completely throw me off balance. After being trained in clinical psychology as well as being a professional coach, I could not believe that I could not get a grip on my feelings, thoughts, fears, and ego. There was something missing that kept me struggling with my emotions even after all the training I received and all the books I have read. Nothing could help me to stop the inward struggle that at times kept me stuck and frustrated. After months of feeling like this and growing tired of it, I allowed myself to listen to my inner voice. This voice told me to write. As I did, the answers and understanding that I was searching for became revealed. This writing evolved into this book, which is my latest eruption.

My latest eruption is my greatest gift, because I have been guided to understand how to work *with our emotions rather than against them*. We must understand our emotions as they were intended and not in all the ways we have been taught. *Our feelings, fears, and even our ego are present to **support** us to live our best life*. We have been misled about our emotions, and when we fully understand the truth of them, we will be on our way to making our life our ideal.

Examine the Ways You Inhibit Your Authentic Expression

Is there a part of my story that sounds familiar? Maybe my story is more dramatic than your life's version, or maybe yours has had even further struggles. Whatever the case, now is the time to begin to acknowledge how you inhibit yourself from being you. When you allow yourself to fully express who you are in the world, you will experience gratitude, joy, and a sense of purpose for living. Instead of feeling frustrated or stuck in life, you will feel in purpose as you flow through each day with greater ease.

In order to create the life you desire, you must be willing to acknowledge how you tend to avoid your feelings. You may invalidate them by saying something like "I cannot be sad. Look at all that I have in life. There is nothing to be sad about." Then you attempt to list all the reasons why you do not have a right to be sad.

You may also be prone to dismissing your feelings altogether. For instance, you may awaken feeling "off." Instead of trying to understand this feeling, you immediately go into focusing on the demands of your day. You may rationalize that how you are feeling is simply due to your life being so busy.

Do you feel like you are on the go from the moment you wake up most mornings? Perfect! You have set it up this way so that you do not have the energy to address your truth. People who are like this tend to need to always be doing something to feel "productive." If they are not being productive, they are numbing themselves out in some way, whether it is through television, the internet, video games, food, or alcohol/drugs.

When we are living our lives in any of these ways that support us to deny our truth, we are not truly living. We are surviving. We are living in survival mode as we are doing all we can to get by. As we know, this is not the way to create a fulfilled life.

The Journey Begins with Acknowledgement

Acknowledgement is always the first and most coura-geous step. So many times I run into people who end up sharing with me how in one way or another they are disap-pointed about their life. Yet they do not see that what they are sharing is their pain. They have bought into the lie that life is just meant to give them a bad deal in one or two or several areas of their life. If they continue to buy into this lie, their life will continue to go downhill until they are in enough pain that they know in their heart that life cannot or should not be this hard.

When we reach the point when we are in intolerable pain, we are coming back to our truth. The truth is life is not supposed to be a persistent struggle. We can make it hard, but it is not supposed to be that way. When we accept that life is meant to be good and acknowledge the pain we are in, we can begin to see beyond our limited version of reality. We can open ourselves to letting go of certain conditions in our life that we accepted as normal.

In our world today, many of us are going about living in an emotionally handicapped way. It is as if we are choosing to go through life with one hand tied behind our back. When we live like this, life feels more difficult than it should. We buy into that living this way is normal because most everyone else we meet has one of their hands tied up as well. Because the majority only utilizes one hand, we accept this as the way life is. There will come a time, however, when most of us begin to realize that not everyone is going about life with their hand tied behind their back. We will see that for a certain few, life is easier. When we are able to recognize this for ourselves, we must ask for support. When we do, we begin to receive.

We do not have to accept life for anything less than being perfect for our Spirit. We have within us all that we need to support us spiritually on our path. We just need to be willing to untie the old bonds that are not serving our highest and greatest good. Just as untying our arm would make our lives physically easier, we will also feel a sense of emotional freedom as we break free from being bound to beliefs that do not serve our highest selves.

In order to support our highest selves, we must first be willing to acknowledge what is not working for us in our lives currently. For many people this is challenging, because they are used to settling for satisfactory. Although they know their life is not exactly as they would like it, they feel overall that their life is not too bad. This mentality is just another form of dismissing pain.

A recent example is of a woman who could easily recognize that she was lonely. She missed not having a relationship after her last boyfriend, yet on some level she just accepted life this way. She was beautiful, successful, and kind, yet she was buying into the mentality that "we can't have it all." It was like she felt no right to complain about her feelings because the other areas of her life were amazing.

When we rationalize our feelings, we are stating to the Universe that we are just fine with how our life is currently when truly we are not. If we want life to be different, we must be willing to admit that our current circumstances are not our ideal. When we are able to share our truth, we open ourselves to new options. The more open we become, the more likely we will be willing to take a risk. Often times our risks are simply our intuition guiding us to create the necessary change. Even though the risk may feel scary to us, we are being guided along the way in order to manifest our ideal life.

Discovering our Truth Is a Journey

When I work with my clients and they become ready to face their truth, they often want a quick fix. They will say to me "Okay, I have admitted that I am lost and lonely. Now how do I get rid of these feelings?" The truth is we are not trying to get rid of our feelings because we need them to understand what we need to do in our life to become balanced again. Learning how to do this takes time, patience, and practice.

As with any part of our lives in which we are led to further develop, we go through phases. When we are infants, we do not start out walking because we need to get an overall feel first for our environment. As we develop that understanding, we begin making progress toward being able to move independently in the world. If we were to learn to move about in our world without having our bearings, we would experience a lot more pain. Thus, we are given phases in our development to ensure our success.

Our emotional understanding needs to develop in the same manner. We work through phases in order that we master an area before we move further to creating our ideal. We must have these emotional skills and understanding established in order to fully be able to manifest all that we desire to create in our life. Hence, we are meant to take baby steps as we move away from devaluing our emotional selves to understanding the guidance our emotions give us. Once we are able to recognize the truth of our emotions, we will know that any time we choose to dismiss how we feel, we are throwing away the abundance in life we say we desire.

Learning the Process Allows for Struggle

Even though I recognize the truth of my emotions, there are still times when I struggle with my feelings. To banish struggling with aspects of our life would miss the point, as sometimes we need that inner struggle to push us forward toward creating the life we desire to have. The key is having moments of struggle rather than feeling like our life in some way feels like a struggle. There is a huge difference. I should know, as I have lived life both ways. I have struggled through life in which each day I felt exhausted, depleted, and bored. "Is this all there is to life?" I often questioned.

Now if I struggle to acknowledge my feelings, it does not last long. I can no longer ignore how I feel for any length of time because I feel off center. Because I trust that my emotions will guide me to finding my center again, I am able to listen to them. Nevertheless, there are moments when I get caught up in the same excuses that keep us all separated from our truth. The difference is being separated from my truth no longer feels like my norm, as I know how good I feel when I make the appropriate adjustments that are guided through my feelings.

A recent example happened a few days ago in which I woke up not feeling myself. I was desperately feeling like I needed to get away. I felt anxious and overwhelmed by the responsibilities I had. By the afternoon, when I was able to get my children to nap, I recognized that I had to address what was bothering me. I listened and was guided to go outside. I got on a swing for a while and then I just lay in the grass. After a while, I decided to start picking up sticks. As I did, I had this overwhelming sense of gratitude for my life. I felt in awe that I had the ability to do this simple task and be a steward to our land. I began to feel extremely connected to the Earth and God. This process lasted two hours, and from that time I no longer felt anxious or overwhelmed or had the need to get away. Furthermore, the next day my ideas flowed out of me and I was able to get my work done with ease and pleasure.

This is how our life works when we are willing to follow the flow of our emotions. How we are guided may not make logical sense, yet if we are willing to trust, we will experience the abundance we desire to have. By abundance, I do not mean only the material items we may desire. I also mean the feeling states of happiness, joy, gratitude, love for life, passion, and purpose. Without these feeling states, our material gains will continue to feel empty. When we live our lives aligned with our truth, we create a life in which we experience abundance from the internal. As we create abundance internally, we will see abundance reflected back to us in the external world we have created.

This book has been created to share with you the phases of the journey of discovering your truth in order that you can *authentically* create your ideal. The chapters are created for you to build upon each skill, one after another. As you begin mastering these skills, you will already begin to notice shifts that are supporting you to move closer to your ideal. This is a real and life-changing process, yet you must be willing to apply yourself to make these changes occur.

When this book comes into your life, know that you are exactly where you are meant to be. It means that you are ready to authentically address your truth in order that you can create magnificent life changes to support you to live your best life. As you go through this shift, have compassion for yourself. You have lived your whole life dismissing the aspects of yourself you did not like, and now you are being shown differently. Remember that creating this shift from within takes time and is a journey. There is no quick fix, yet the effort you put toward discovering your truth will come back to you in more ways than you can ever imagine!

Putting this Chapter into Practice:

1) Begin to notice your language. Sometimes we do not even realize how we feel about our life. What language are you choosing when people ask you "How are you doing?" Is your reply is "Okay, fine, or all right?" If so, what is inhibiting you from saying that your life is great? That is your key to understanding your feelings. I still utilize this tool for myself. If I keep answering that I feel tired or busy, then I hear how I am not feeling balanced currently in my life. By paying attention to our language, we can depict our truth and create the necessary changes to live a life that feels joyful and balanced.

2) Slow yourself down. Give yourself time to reconnect with you. Take time to go for a walk outside, turn off the radio in the car, don't call anyone, and stay away

from the television or computer for awhile to give yourself more time to reflect. See what type of answer you receive as you ask to be open to discovering all that you are meant to be expressing of yourself at this time.

3) Drink water. It may sound funny, yet there is a connection between our body, mind, and Spirit. What we put in our body impacts our emotions. Water is clear and cleansing, which will support our emotions to flow through us. Just drinking more water will make you feel better as you know you are properly nurturing yourself as well.

Chapter 2
Knowing and Honoring Our Inner Voice

Many people ask me half jokingly, "Am I crazy?" when they admit to all the voices they hear in their heads. Of course, they do not feel too crazy because they are able to function well enough in the world. Still, they wonder "What voice is it that I am hearing and talking back to all the time in my head?" "Is it a voice I should listen to or not?"

In order to continuing moving in the direction we desire toward optimal living, we need to more deeply examine our internal dialogue processes. In this chapter, we will gain further clarity toward being able to differentiate between our inner voice and our ego. Once we are able to recognize our inner voice, we will feel freed from much of the inner talk from the ego, which tends to be extremely judgmental. Through knowing what our soul speaks, we will move toward being able to fully own the power and magnificence that is innately within each of us.

Which Voice Is Which?

At first when we are trying to listen to our inner voice, it feels lost amidst other, maybe even more familiar, voices in our mind. Our inner voice speaks the truth to our essence, or Spirit. Our inner voice is there, trying to get across what is best for us, but it is overrun by our fears, ego, and rational mind. These other voices are disguises of the ego. They are trying to give the illusion that we have control over our life. We do have some control: to either make choices that are congruent with our Spirit or to choose against our Spirit.

Nevertheless, whichever way we choose, we still do not have control over the exact outcome. The beauty is that when we choose to follow our Spirit, the outcome exceeds our expectations, as it is beyond what we could have ever imagined.

One simple way to know the difference between our Spirit and our mind/ego is if we have a desire, yet we keep running up against reasons why we cannot or should not act on it. The voice of our Spirit is sharing with us our desires, while our mind/ego is trying to keep us trapped by creating reasons, which feel very real, as to why we cannot do what our Spirit is telling us to do.

Learning to free ourselves from too much mind clutter will allow our inner voice to come through more clearly. Clearing away the clutter in our mind means that we need to purposefully learn to shut off the process of "thinking things through" when we face a dilemma. We can begin by giving our desires a chance. When we think of desire, we may be thinking of our passions. Many people may feel they do not have a clue what their passions are, which is not surprising if they have not been listening to their inner voice. This is okay. Trust me, we all find our passions once we begin to listen more and more to our inner voice.

Desires do not have to necessarily be about our passion. We can have a desire to tell someone how we truly feel, to take a trip, or to treat ourselves nicely in some way. This is our inner voice. Listening to this voice is not only nurturing to ourselves, but it also gives us practice with allowing ourselves to be guided. As we continue to accept this guidance, we will be open enough to allow into our lives our true passions.

For many, the struggle between our mind and Spirit feels like a battle within us. Some people even feel this physically in their stomach, which is why we have expressions such as "my stomach is tied up in knots." Our stomach becomes "tied up in knots" because we are wrestling around with those ideas in that area of our body. The fight is between honoring our truth versus being controlled by our fears. This fight is fought in the stomach because that is where we carry our energy regarding self-worth and listening to our will. We will find that once we resolve the issue in favor of our Spirit, our stomach issues will go away.

There is another difference between our ego and Spirit. Our ego is the voice that will tell us we *should* be taking some sort of action or *should* be feeling a certain way that we do not. When our inner voice is guiding us, we authentically feel compelled to act. This feeling of being drawn to act gives us the motivation to manifest what we desire, regardless of whether or not our mind can comprehend how it will happen. Furthermore, our emotions will be verifying that our inner voice is guiding us, because we will feel good when we do act on our desire. When we feel manipulated by our ego to act out of guilt or desire to meet our ego's need, we will not feel good.

Can we sense the difference in energy between feeling we should act versus being drawn to move? Of course we can, and so do other people. People can sense the heaviness and weight of our energy when we give out of obligation. We also sense the lightness and uplifting energy when we are giving because we feel inspired to do so.

We can trust that our Spirit will nudge us to make movements each and every day to support us to live life more easily and in a more fulfilling way. This occurs, for example, when a reminder just pops into our head. All of sudden we will think of something out of nowhere that we need to take care of. It is in our best interest to follow that guidance. Even if our mind thinks that the guidance does not make sense or the matter can be taken care of later, we will be happy we listened.

Learning to Trust the Guidance We Receive from Our Inner Voice

Learning to trust the voice within us is being able to recognize that when we listen to God's wisdom and guidance, the perfect solution will occur. If our gut is telling us we do not want to do something, this is our inner guidance. Otherwise we are assuming we are wiser than God when we question and refute the guidance we are being given. Unfortunately, many of us do that all the time because we do not have faith yet in the power within each of us due to our connection to our Source.

We must understand that when we act because we *think* we should, we are really doing a disservice. (*Think* is the operative word, because it demonstrates that it is our mind trying to overrun our inner voice). When we act because we think we should do something (rather than authentically feeling drawn to take action), in actuality we are taking away the opportunity for the perfect solution to occur. If we are not feeling the desire within to act, we must believe it is for good reason. God may be bringing the perfect person *who does feel compelled within* to help. That person's support will then be perfect for her or him, because that person will gain this experience, which is important for her or his growth. The bottom line is that we must have just as much faith in those times when we are guided not to act as we do when we are guided to act. Otherwise, our actions risk being based on our ego rather than our inner voice.

"What if no one volunteers to act when someone needs help?" I've heard my clients worry. The outcome may not turn out to be what the person in need desires, but it is a part of their spiritual journey. Even though the experience may prove to be painful, we can trust that a wealth of spiritual growth and wisdom is available to those impacted. The Universe's reasoning could be endless, and we cannot always understand the Universe's plan. What we can understand, if we are willing to listen, is the wisdom and guidance our Source gives each of us through our inner voice.

We know that if we follow the guidance of our inner voice, we will feel balanced, good, and in alignment with our truth. If we do not follow our guidance when we are told to give, we risk becoming depleted to do our life's work and purpose. Rather than listening to our gut and what our Spirit is guiding us to do, we are busying ourselves with too many obligations. On the other hand, when our gut is telling us to offer support and we decline out of fear, lack of energy, or for whatever reason, we will not feel fulfilled.

Learning to Check In Rather than Continue to Check Out

It is our responsibility to check in with ourselves, especially when we are facing a decision. If we are hesitating, then we need to listen, because our Spirit is trying to guide us to do something different than our typical or automatic response would have us do. Many people question, "What if I never want to help someone?" That is just our fear speaking to us. Many people fear they will never want to give because they are so overextended that they deeply desire a break! Once we allow ourselves that break, we will have renewed energy to give toward the areas that matter to our hearts the most.

Being the Martyr Serves No One!

We have this martyrdom mentality that we are supposed to overextend ourselves. However, if we look at the people whom we look up to because they were martyrs, they were martyrs because their heart was their driving force. Their heart filled them with passion and energy toward giving to their purpose, not in every area of life.

When I think of a person who was able to give endlessly from her heart, Mother Teresa comes to mind. Her giving heart was so pure and full of love that she touched millions. She gave her energy toward the people she was drawn to support. Her life allowed her to maintain focus on her primary purpose for giving. Would Mother Teresa have been able to touch as many people if she chose to have a family? Not likely. We need to see that people's lives were set up to be able to give to a certain degree, which is impacted by their circumstances. The degree is based on that which will give us the greatest amount of happiness and joy we desire to experience in the many areas of life that are important to us. We were not given our purpose to feel overwhelmed and stressed out. Therefore, if we chose to have multitude of aspects that are all a part of our purpose, part of our journey is to find the correct balance that brings us joy and peace. In order for any of us to find balance, peace, and joy in life, we need to listen to the guidance of our Spirit and trust it.

If our Spirit is not guiding us to act, then we are not supposed to be the giver this time. Wait. Wait to see what our Spirit really has in store for us. Maybe it will be time for relaxation and restoring our energy. Maybe we will be guided to put our energy elsewhere. If we do wait and listen, our giving will feel authentic, energized, and full of passion for what we are doing. No longer will our giving lead us to resentful or depleted feelings, which is often the case when we give out of obligation.

When we do something out of a sense of obligation, we are better not doing so because we truly are not present. When we do not want to be in a certain situation, this is because our Spirit has a better notion of what would be good for us. If we go along with what our ego tells us we should do, we often check out and are not really "there" anyway. If this is our continuous pattern, then we are not truly present in our life. This is not living the way we are intended to live. Being present and listening to our hearts' desires allows us to live fully in each moment.

Allowing Our Inner Voice to Provide the Nurturance We Need to Create Our Desires

In order to be present and hear our inner voice clearly, we need to learn to take care of our souls. Nurturing and caring for ourselves means taking care of the basics, such as getting enough sleep, exercising, and eating well. Nurturing ourselves also involves doing activities that fuel our soul and uplift our Spirit. For me, this means swinging on a swing, dancing, singing, painting, and being in nature. Giving myself time to relax, rest, or converse with God and the loving Spirits that surround me always feels nurturing and supportive.

Many people I know have struggled with allowing themselves this time as they told me, "To sit still means that I am not accomplishing anything." By society's standards, this may be true, but certainly from a spiritual viewpoint, we are living in purpose when we allow ourselves to refuel our Spirit. We then need to decide which standard is better for us in the long run and which will make us happier, more joyful, and full of life. If the standard we choose is not working for us, then why would we continue to go about life in the same manner?

My life coach once told me, "It is insanity to do the same thing over and over while expecting different results." When we are not happy and full of joy, appreciation, and love for living, then we need to be willing to change. Switch it up. By daring ourselves to take new steps toward our self-care, we can observe the results for ourselves. Observe how we would have felt if we continued to act how we usually do compared to how we feel when we allow ourselves to follow our inner guidance.

We need to remember that it will always feel good to nurture and care for ourselves when that is what our Spirit is telling us to do. When our Spirit wants us to take action rather than relax, we will feel that as well. We do not need our voice of guilt to tell us what to do. We have an inner voice that is there to guide us for our highest good. Our guilt, on the other hand, is that voice that tries to keep us small and wants to keep control over us. God would not make us feel bad for caring for ourselves if that is what our soul desires. Remember, if we are all made from God's essence, then caring for ourselves is demonstrating our reverence and love to God for giving us this precious life to live.

Often times I plead with clients to give their inner voice a chance. Their Spirit is begging to be heard, as it needs to be nourished. What their Spirit desires is often so obvious, yet their egos are trying to keep them boxed in doing what they are *supposed* to do. Excuse after excuse will come to them from their ego why it is not possible to simply listen to their hearts' longings. If they give their Spirit a chance, my clients always see how easily their life comes together in order for them to manifest their desires. When they allow this to happen, they are remembering the truth, which is when we are aligned with our Spirit, everything will fall into place with ease. The Universal energies are always ready to support us to become in alignment with our soul. For this reason, what may have seemed impossible or conflictive on the physical plane is easily overcome on the spiritual plane.

One of my clients yearned to get away and visit her family, as it was a place that felt very renewing to her feminine Spirit. Of course, she had many excuses as to why it could not happen. I told her she had a choice to either remain depleted, anxious, and full of worry about everyday life, or she could listen to what her soul was longing for and take the trip. She recognized that her soul was longing for this, but time felt like it was an issue, since her children would be starting school in a few days. Additionally, she did not want to spend much money on such a short trip. I told her that her Spirit was desperately asking for her to listen and nurture herself. Furthermore, I reminded her if she listened to her Spirit and asked for support, she would receive it. I concluded with stating that she either needed to make this trip happen, the best choice, or put it in the books within the next couple of months.

At our next meeting, I saw before me a new person. Before my client even told me, I knew she was able to get away as her soul desired. Her soul seemed freer, happier, and more at peace even though she was back to running around taking care of the needs of her three young children. I asked her how she made the trip happen. She said with amazement how easily all the logistics came together for her. She used frequent flyer miles in an account that only had enough miles for one ticket. Furthermore, she was able to go during just the time frame that she hoped. She was surprised at how it all came together and that she actually had the courage to make it happen. I reminded her that this is how easy life will be when she continues to listen to her Spirit and trusts in the guidance she receives rather than fighting what her Spirit is telling her to do.

Our Fear of Taking Care of Ourselves

Some of my clients worry that they will become too self-centered by taking care of themselves and listening to their inner voice. They only feel this way, however, because they are so depleted. It feels for them and for many people that they could go on nurturing themselves for eternity. This is good, because we all should. However, what we fail to realize is once we nurture ourselves and therefore restore our soul, we will be open to further guidance.

When we regain our energy, we can be guided as to what it is that our soul truly desires us to do. Often times this is some sort of service or giving. In other instances, we gain renewed energy and perspective for our present work. Again, this is part of having the trust and faith in our Spirit and inner voice to guide us. Our ego tells us to worry about being too selfish. Our inner Spirit, however, will guide us toward creating the perfect balance for our soul, which includes both nurturance for ourselves and service to others.

Shedding Light on Our Guilt

Even with the understanding that we can only truly be present and give from our heart when our needs are cared for, most people I know still struggle with guilt. When I forget my truth, I can as well. We buy into our guilt because it has been ingrained into our minds that self-care equates to selfishness. In order to address our guilt, we need to understand the facts about selfishness.

Selfishness is about being inconsiderate of other people's needs and/or feelings. The truth is that we become unable to relate and be considerate of others when we become disconnected from our own needs and feelings. In other words, when we lack compassion for ourselves, we lack compassion for others. Furthermore, when we become disconnected from our truth and the basic requirements of nurturing our body, mind, and soul, we become lost. We have lost our grounding by not providing ourselves with our basic needs. Instead of nurturing ourselves, we attempt to control the world around us, including the people and events that make up our lives.

When we look outside ourselves to try to attain acceptance, value, and worth, we are acting selfishly by trying to control others and events around us to fulfill our needs. However, when we meet our own needs by giving ourselves the requirements we need on a body, mind, and soul level, we are fulfilled. We do not have to look to others for our fulfillment, and therefore we are able to give of ourselves authentically, as we were meant to do. When we are able to give of ourselves in this effortless manner is when we will have the energy, drive, and focus to put toward our passions. When we focus our energy on our passion, we create the life we desire to live. This all begins with the willingness to know that we require and deserve nurturance of our body, mind, and soul in order to live rather than just to survive.

The perfect example of how we are unconsciously selfish when we are not in our truth is my experience throughout my twenties. Because I felt completely lost at that time, I did not truly know myself, and my inner voice was buried. During that time in my life, I was a neurotic control freak. I wanted to control events around me so they looked perfect, which in turn would make me feel like I was perfect, too. I wanted people to like and admire me so that I would feel a sense of worth. In other words, I was using people as a means to the end of having my needs fulfilled.

At the time, I would have never recognized my behavior as selfish. In my mind, I was trying my hardest to be a good person. In fact, I was often trying to please everyone. How on earth can this be selfish? When we try to please others, we are trying to manipulate them in order to serve our needs. Manipulating others to meet our own needs is selfish regardless of whether our manipulation feels good or bad to them. Once we are attuned to our true self, we know that there is no such need to "try" to be a good person. We innately are living to our highest potential when we follow our inner voice. Once we provide our needs for ourselves, it no longer feels good to us to get our needs met external to ourselves. Providing for our internal needs feels empowering, peaceful, and loving. When we search outside ourselves, we cause ourselves pain by continuing to push our inner voice down, while at the same time, we hurt others, as we are using them to meet our needs.

The other gift in providing for our own internal needs is that the process allows us to gain compassion for ourselves. We gain compassion when we turn to old behaviors to try to fulfill a need externally rather than trust our inner voice. As we are able to step back and witness ourselves and our actions, we become empathetic toward others when they go through the same struggle. Gaining compassion for ourselves allows us to have further compassion, love, and understanding for others. Furthermore, as we consider our needs more often and how good it feels to attend to them, we are better able to recognize the same needs in others. In other words, the act of nurturing and caring for ourselves allows us to put energy toward ourselves when necessary and then frees our energy to be aware of others in our lives. When we do not attend to our needs, our energy is subconsciously being focused on ourselves continuously, which means we are not living presently with others in our lives. Hence, we only need to worry about becoming selfish when we are not willing to listen to our inner guidance and truth.

Guilt Is Not How God Communicates to Us

God's voice is never guilt. We may feel like we are being nudged, even pushed along sometimes in our guidance, yet this is still different than the ego. Guilt is part of the ego trying to control us, belittle us, and tell us what bad people we are if we do not follow its commands. We must always remember there is a difference between what our ego believes is the right thing to do and what is right for our Spirit.

If we still get confused, we can always check back in with our emotions. If we feel we are being guided to do something but not sure if it is coming from our ego or our Spirit, how do we feel when we picture ourselves going through with the guidance? If we feel at ease and peaceful or a smile comes on our face, it is our Spirit guiding us. If we feel dread and distaste wash over us, this is our ego trying to convince us we should take action in order that we "do the right thing." God already knows that we are inherently good. The difference is that *we* will know we are good when we begin listening to our Spirit. If you are curious as to how much guilt is impacting your life, go to www.michellebersell.com and take my free quiz.

Creating Support in Our Lives Frees Our Inner Voice

So many people are reluctant to get help when it can support them to manifest their hearts' desires. After seeing so many friends, clients, and myself struggle with asking for help, it is important for me to emphasize that it is integral to get the support we need to make our lives better. Whether this help is a life coach, babysitter, dog walker, therapist, lawn service, maid, personal trainer, nutritionist–get it now in order to feel free to truly live in greatness. None of us can live life fully if we are overwhelmed with personal anguish. Neither can we truly live life if we are overwhelmed with a mile-long to-do list every day. By giving ourselves support in the areas where we feel overwhelmed, we are giving ourselves the nurturance that our soul requires in order for us to live our life with joy and passion.

I know many of you may be saying to yourselves, "Sure, that would be great Michelle, but who is going to pay for it?" We can all afford to make some sort of change that will free us up in some manner. First, we must set our intentions that this can come into our lives affordably. Second, we must check our priorities. Are we throwing our money out the window each day on items that do not necessarily uplift our Spirit such as cable television, gossipy magazines, or a cup of joe on the go when we could easily make coffee in our home? Is our money better spent on being able to support ourselves rather than eating lunch out every day? Each of us must determine for ourselves where we are willing to shift our spending, because for each of us it will be different. Our long-term happiness is worth becoming more conscious of how we spend our money. Money is only energy, and we want our energy to reflect that which our heart desires. If how we spend does not reflect our desires, we need to make some changes.

For some people, even though they have some extra money to spend each month, they do not feel worthy of spending it on themselves. Their mentality is to spend money on the basics, so spending on anything else would be reckless. Their focus is on saving for the future. What people do not get is that our mental health should be part of our basics. I do not want people to start spending out of control or on need-less items at the shopping mall. Yes, that may be fun for us to do every so often, but that will not keep us fueled with energy and a sense of balance. It is imperative to our spiritual and emotional health to give ourselves time to "be" rather than "do." If we want to live a life full of passion, then we must be willing to free ourselves of the overwhelming "to-do" lists.

Many people understand the need to care for themselves but do not feel deserving enough to give themselves such a "luxury." We need to ask ourselves if taking care of more than our physical needs should be considered a luxury. We also need to question ourselves if we are here simply to survive or to live a full, joyful, and peaceful life. Many of us go through each day in survival mode. We need to recognize that we will only lead a rich life if we are willing to put the energy toward getting the necessary support we need to make it happen.

Time and money are both sources of our energy, as both depict our focus in life. Hence, we need to examine how we are currently utilizing our time and money. Is our energy going toward what we say matters most to us in life? Many people say what is important to them is God, their families, spouse, children, friends, and health. However, their time and money is not being spent on these areas of their life. Instead, it is disproportionately going toward our careers, television viewing, internet surfing, etc. This is our clue then that we are not living life according to what is best for our highest good. Instead, we are just surviving.

We must be clear that we will never find "discretionary" time or money in order to make our life fulfilling to us. With all our heart, mind, and soul, we must become committed to living life to our fullest. Only we can make it happen for ourselves. Otherwise, I guarantee that it will never occur. Through demonstrating our willingness to change our focus from surviving to living, we will see our lives shift to living a more joyful, passionate, and loving existence.

Still, there are times in most everyone's lives in which finding funds to support their path will be more challenging than other times. If this is the case, we can still ask for abundance through creative solutions in the areas where we desire more support. Many of the stay-at-home moms I knew felt they were in this dilemma due to losing the income they previously brought to their families. They also felt that life was meant to be tough during the time they were raising their children. Knowing that this thinking was hindering mothers, I set out to have discussions with them to support moms to know there is another way if we ask for help, regardless of our financial situation.

Some of the moms I met with took what I said to heart and vowed to create more time for themselves in their lives. These were not wealthy women; many had budgets to contend with, but they found a way to make it happen. Some moms asked kids who were not old enough to babysit yet were interested in helping out with their kids. These young girls provided a lot of support, even though they were too young to be left alone with small children. While learning to manage children, these young girls allowed the mom to take some time to herself. It was a win-win, as each person was getting what she desired. The mom was able to get a little bit of a break and the mother's helpers were gaining experience in order to be able to know how to babysit for children in the future. To top it off, no money was exchanged!

Other moms swapped their children on certain days or asked the grandparents for more help. Once they created the support they needed, these women could not imagine living life as it had been. They felt more energized as they gave themselves the time to breathe, relax, and nurture themselves by taking walks or a yoga class, or sitting down and reading a book. Doing this for themselves at least once a week did wonders. They came back to their life with such more life force and happiness to be with their children. This is how life should be.

In order for these women to create this change, they also made another change, which I suggest for everyone as she creates the life she desires. They only surrounded themselves with mothers who believed mothering could be enjoyable. This meant that they had to let go of those connections with mothers who only wanted to complain and discuss how difficult life is raising their children. We all recognize that raising kids is challenging and being able to discuss those challenges is pertinent to caregivers. However, the difference in the agenda of the caregivers is between those who desire their experience to be joyful and those whose focus is on how difficult it is for them.

We all need to surround ourselves with others who are on the same path. We need other people to positively reinforce that we can manifest our desires. Otherwise, if we choose to receive input from others that suggests we cannot manifest our best life, it is too easy to fall back into old patterns that do not serve our highest good.

All we need to do is to support one another in being able to make an initial small shift. I am happy to be that person people come to when they want to know if it is okay to "indulge" in some way, whether it is a chocolate truffle, a new pair of shoes, or a spa treatment. They know if they come to me, I will say, "Go for it!" This is because I know that their soul is longing to be nurtured. Most of the people I know are not overindulgent. Rather, they are so controlled that they do not trust within themselves when it is okay to let go.

Many people's big fear is, "If I let go of controlling, I am afraid I will become out of control!" We only sense that we will become out of control when we do not have balance in our lives. If we never give ourselves that piece of chocolate, the pair of shoes we adore, or the nurturance we crave, we will feel depleted and imbalanced. If we take care of ourselves and our needs, then we will find that balance.

What we do not realize is that what our soul is asking for in order to feel nurtured is usually so small. The other day I "indulged" on $8 liquid soap rather than $1 liquid soap. Usually I am a practical type of shopper. Yet on this day, my

Spirit thought it would feel good to use a nicely made and beautifully fragrant soap. Each day I use it, I feel good. My point is that what we do for our soul does not have to be a big deal or even cost money. The point is that we tell our Spirit that we are willing to care for and love ourselves. Once we do those small acts, our energy and passion for living multiplies.

We will only go off the deep end if there are other issues taking us away from our truth. If that is the case, we start utilizing "indulgences" as a means to cope with what is bothering us. This is why people overeat, shop excessively, or exhibit any behavior in an imbalanced manner. By being aware of our fears and emotions, which we will address in the upcoming chapters, we do not need to fear becoming overindulgent because we are aligned with our Spirit.

Regardless of our monetary status, we can make changes that will support us to live our best life. We only need to know that we deserve to do so and have the power to create that change. Commit to make any change today, small or big, and you will see the benefits each and every day after.

Creativity is Not Optional

I was almost orgasmic yesterday as I started to paint. Picking up my paintbrush felt that good! It had been a couple of months since I had painted, and my soul was desperately craving for me to create in this way. Although I had been expressing myself creatively in different ways, I felt an inner *need* to paint again. The feeling of expression I get in being able to transform a blank canvas to something that depicts a part of me feels heavenly. To me, painting feels like freedom.

The excitement that washes over me when I paint is a more recent experience in my life. In fact, I used to have a deep fear about any artistic expression due to an art teacher's critical judgment of my work in middle school. She felt I was not trying hard enough. She was right, but it was not because I was being oppositional - it was because I was afraid. Most everything else I put effort into would turn out well. If I studied, I did well on tests. Drawing or other forms of art, on the other hand, never turned out exactly as I expected. Thus, whenever I did any form of art, I usually felt disappointed in the end.

Unfortunately, my art teacher did not recognize my fear. Rather, she heightened my reluctance toward art by critiquing my work. I thought it would be better from an ego standpoint to get a bad grade in art because I did not try. Otherwise if I really tried, I would not only feel bad because I did not like what I created but also because I got a bad grade, too. Unfortunately, three years with this teacher in middle school made me vow to stay away from anything artistic. In my mind, I had labeled myself as not being creative.

Judging my creativity shut down a large part of my feminine side. Feeling like "I did not have a creative bone in my body" made me focus more on my analytical skills. My analytical skills were also those most prized by society and those that would help me become successful, so I was told. The problem was that this was not my truth. I was creative, just not in a typical-art-class-kind-of-way. Nevertheless, I carried this stigma around for years, limiting what I would attempt based on my judgment about not being creative.

As I began to awaken to my truth, I could recognize that I had bought into our analytical world too much and had forsaken my femininity. I did not even know what it really meant to be feminine. In my mind, being feminine meant "getting dolled up," which equated to putting on makeup, a dress, and high heels. That was it! I had no idea of what it meant to own my feminine strengths or that there even were feminine strengths. The interesting aspect to this perspective is that I did not come from a patriarchal family. My mother was very strong. She was the one who made the majority of the decisions in our family, had the checkbook, and ran a business with my father. Nevertheless, I still felt confused as I began to ask myself questions about being feminine. "What are the feminine traits that are valued? What was a feminine realm of success? What did it mean to own my femininity?" I wondered.

The truth is that we all have feminine and masculine aspects. Because the masculine tends to be more valued in most societies, many of us have lost balance. This has been at a cost to our world, especially to women, for many women have lost a part of who we are. Nevertheless, whether we are a woman or a man, if there is not societal value in what we have to offer from within ourselves, we are less likely to express our talents, viewpoints, and creativity.

Many people look at expressing ourselves creatively as discretionary. Usually when we view something as optional, we do not exercise that option. How could we when we have so many other tasks to complete? For women in particular who are raising their families, some working outside their home, and taking care of their household duties, there is no discretionary time for creativity, let alone sleep! Yet we view our creativity as discretionary because we do not recognize the value in expressing ourselves in an artistic manner.

All of us need to allow our creative juices to flow. If we do not, we become stagnant. Expressing our creativity gives us the feeling that we are truly living, because we are sharing a part of our souls. So many people I have met lack passion, which is because they continue to view expressing themselves creatively as more or less a waste of their time. The truth is that not expressing ourselves creatively is *more* of a waste of our lives. Why? If we do not express our creativity, we are remaining too analytical. Being in our heads will not lead us to our passions. We need to be willing to connect with our soul, our heart, and our inner child to awaken to all that life has to offer. By connecting from within, we are able to play. Being free to play allows room for inspiration and passion.

Ask yourself, is living without inspiration and passion really living? Now determine if expressing yourself creatively is still optional. I guarantee you it is not.

The problem is that many people feel stuck as to how to begin expressing themselves creatively. The reality is that we are creating all the time because everything we do is a creation. Our thoughts, beliefs, and ideas are all creations. The simple tasks of our day are creations. Washing the dishes, making a meal, taking out the garbage, defining our space in our homes or office, or deciding on our clothes, hairstyle, and make-up are all creations. They utilize a part of our creativity, because we chose how to go about doing these things in our life.

Once we begin to honor the magnitude in all that we create, we will be able to own the power we have to create in all areas of our life. We can become more playful with how we take out the trash. We can create more variety in the ingredients we use in a favorite dish or in the color of make-up we choose. The options to utilizing creativity in our lives are endless! As we begin to play with our creativity in our every day endeavors, we will see our inspiration ignite other aspects of our lives. Begin to look at your life as a canvas that you have the ability to change and make more playful.

My husband, who does not believe he has a creative bone in his body, is very creative, especially when it comes to food. He tells everyone that he does not and cannot cook. This is not true. He does not cook by any traditional means, but he does make some very interesting and sometimes tasty food concoctions. He has a knack for finding all sorts of different variety of foods, putting them together in a tortilla, and making a meal out of it. Although mostly not to my taste, he and my kids love it! This is a form of creativity for him.

Remember, I too did not think I had any creativity within me, but this, of course, was not true either. I used to love decorating my home and utilize a lot of creativity doing so just by figuring out the placement of my furniture or determining what knick-knacks speak about me and my family. Recognizing my daily duties as a time where I could add some play also made my tasks more fun and creative. For instance, looking at cooking as a creative endeavor also loosened me up to try new recipes or to not use a recipe at all and experiment with food instead. If a meal does not turn out, who cares? Allowing myself this freedom taught me to be less in a hurry, as well as less judgmental, about all that I do. I can do my household chores and have everything be perfect, or I can go about my daily tasks and have more fun with life even though I may get less done. I have found that utilizing my energy creatively can be more time consuming when completing a task, but in the end, I have gained more time and energy. How? Because I decided to allow myself time to play. When I choose this, I am happy and therefore have more energy to put toward taking care of the tasks that need to get done.

By allowing myself to see my daily living as a creative endeavor, I opened myself up to expressing myself artistically again in a more traditional manner. The key for me was learning not to be so critical of what I create. Through my new perception of creativity, I let down my guard and picked up a colored pencil. I did not try to create anything concrete, as that had brought me too much frustration in the past. Instead, I just played. From there I picked up paint, clay, markers, or anything that allowed me to play artistically. What I found was that I had a wonderful ability to combine color. My art would definitely be considered abstract, but it feels beautiful to me. Having this feeling in and of itself was a huge accomplishment for me.

Now I also experiment with doing some concrete images as well just so I can practice seeing the beauty in all that I create. Just because it is not conventional or others do not see the beauty does not mean that my work is not beautiful. I have learned to view all my art as beautiful because it is an expression of me. I appreciate all my paintings because it helps me to reflect on my experience at certain points in my life. From those paintings, I honor my growth and all the guidance I have been given in order for me to create the woman I am today.

Through being willing to take the chance to express ourselves in a creative way, we open ourselves up to take more risks in life. Creativity is about following our gut, and that is what is going to lead us to living our life filled with passion. Passion for living does not just happen. It takes people who are willing to do whatever it takes in order that their soul will be expressed. Our soul's expression begins with our everyday living and how we choose to create our journey. From there, we continue to expand on expressing ourselves in other areas of life. Through this practice with self-expression, we are preparing ourselves to share our passions with the world.

Choose to no longer look at your self-care as discretionary; otherwise, you may come to see that your life felt like a waste of time. The only waste would be to never express what is within you. Begin by creating the time for you to express yourself artistically in any way and honor it as a creative expression of you. Only you can create the time and make it happen by owning that this is significant to your living. Express yourself in as many different ways as possible, and the world will be blessed.

Continuing to Create the Space Our Inner Voice Needs

There are numerous gifts to our willingness to express ourselves creatively. As mentioned above, our creativity is the fuel for our passion. The other aspect of our creativity is that if we allow ourselves to create without judgment, our inner voice is given the space to express our feelings, thoughts, and needs. As we become accustomed to following the guidance of our inner voice, we will awaken to hearing its whispers more and more. We simply need to create more space in which our minds are not in the lead.

When my inner voice was ready to take the lead, I began to get this feeling within me during the middle of the night that told me to get up because it was time to write. It was a sensation in my stomach, a tingling, a sense of excitement. This initially started to occur when I was completely exhausted and did not want to move. Sometimes I did not get up, but I learned what I was missing out on when I chose to ignore this feeling.

When I am awakened in the middle of the night, I now know it is my Spirit talking to me, telling me there is more for me to share. Sometimes I start hearing the words I am supposed to write while I still lie asleep in bed. Then I know I really need to get up, because if I do not, I will be missing a divine opportunity.

Listening to this sensation on a more or less regular basis is new for me. I used to try to ignore these types of sensations simply because I valued my sleep so much. I did not recognize that these were divine opportunities. It felt more like a nuisance, and I would question, "Why couldn't I sleep?" I began to realize if I would get up, journal, and release the emotions or thoughts on paper, I would feel more at ease. So instead of tossing and turning, I could go back to bed. Soon when I awoke in the middle of the night, I began journaling over a certain dilemma or challenge I was currently facing. I was thrilled to find that when I wrote, I would find my truth, even if I was previously confused. My writing gave me peace, and I found clarity and resolution to my dilemmas. It became a healing activity for me whenever there was something on my mind I could not release. This did not happen all the time, yet it was valuable for me to learn to listen to that voice within me that not only wanted but needed to speak to me.

Now, I have learned, this voice wants to speak not only when I am facing a dilemma but all the time. The voice I came to know through my journaling was my inner voice. Through journaling, my inner voice, rather than my rational voice, was able to speak and be heard. I needed to still my mind enough in order for this voice to be heard. For this reason, it was not until about 4:30 a.m. that my mind was in enough of a fog that my inner voice could come through clearly. Although the time was inconvenient, I knew that this is when I am still and at peace enough to actually receive the Divine Guidance that is flowing through me. "Be still and know that I am" is a verse that shares the way to remembering our truth.

With three young kids–my daughter was three-and-a-half-years old and my twin sons two–4:30 a.m. was the perfect time for me to learn to receive. At this time, I was not being bombarded with requests or needing to patrol their interactions while trying to get done the numerous tasks that needed to get accomplished throughout the day. It is probably one of the few times I was not multitasking! Thus, that time was sacred to me. We need to look for ourselves to find those times in which we allow ourselves to be released from all the responsibilities we face each and every day in order that something miraculous can take place within us. By beginning to honor that time, we can all hear more clearly the guidance of our inner voice.

Through Creating "Downtime," Our Inner Voice Has More Opportunity to Guide Us

Through learning to listen to my inner voice and appreciating all the guidance I have received, my inner guidance now comes throughout the day. Nevertheless, the guidance and wisdom I receive is most easy to hear when I create the time and space for my mind to be open and clear of distractions. Creating "downtime" in which I am either focused on receiving or nurturing my Spirit are important for supporting my inner voice to be heard. The key aspect of downtime is that I am allowing myself to just be.

As a society, we are learning to give ourselves more time to do activities we find enjoyable. We know we need time to release daily stress by exercising or fueling a passion by getting lost in a hobby we enjoy. These are very important for us. Yet just the thought of giving ourselves the time to "just be" makes some people feel uncomfortable. Allowing ourselves to "just be" is when we permit ourselves time to slow down, sit, daydream, and soak in life. We have become so over-programmed with creating activities to busy ourselves that most people feel they cannot "just be."

The damage in not allowing ourselves time to focus on our soul occurs not only to our own Spirit but to our children's Spirit as well. Children today have lost the freedom to just be themselves, imagine, and play because their lives have become programmed as well. There are all sorts of lessons small children can now take, such as music, foreign language, or sports. There is nothing wrong with these classes in and of themselves. The harm, however, is that our society has infiltrated our minds to believe that if we posses all these skills, we will then be special. The truth is that we actually lose our sense of feeling special, as all our energy becomes consumed in our activities.

When we are overdoing, we are so lost in a whirlwind of activity that we have no or little idea about what truly fuels us and brings us a sense of passion. We go along with what everyone else is interested in or involved in because of our fears that if we too do not possess some extra skill or talent, then "what would I have to offer?" This is exactly why so many people feel lost as to what will make them happy. In other words, people are working so hard to "be somebody" that they have lost who they actually are. This is a big loss to our planet and our world.

Avoiding time to relax and wonder about life actually robs us of the true potential that lies within us. If we are overwhelmed with activity in our lives, we are avoiding living fully in our truth. We enjoy golfing, shopping, gambling, drinking, socializing, watching television, surfing the net, reading books, taking another class, talking in chat rooms or over the phone, etc, which in balance is fine. None of these

activities in and of themselves is bad or wrong, but how we
rely on having activity after activity in our life is.

We must remember that we are human *beings* first, not
human *doings*. If we would allow ourselves to "just be," we
would be living our lives to our fullest potential. Unfortunately, most people feel lost as to why they were put here on
earth or what their purpose is. We must realize how difficult
it is to understand our purpose when we put no time aside for
ourselves. Allowing ourselves to just be, slow down, and
daydream is when those magical moments occur. Through
giving ourselves this time, Spirit is allowed in to inspire us.
It is when "ah-ha" moments occur.

This is my dare for anyone: watch the magic unfold when
you are willing to listen to your soul's desires. The Universe
is waiting and willing to be of assistance to all of us when it
comes to supporting us on our life's journey. Take the
assistance, please, as it will be better not only for yourself but
for your family, and for society as well. Be the model of what
it is like to live in Spirit, and others will follow. It is conta-
gious. All you have to do is trust!

Putting this Chapter into Practice:

1) Choose one way to indulge your Spirit this week. Be
   conscious of how giving yourself this gift impacts
   you. Allow yourself to continue acting on those
   nudges when your Spirit desires nurturance. Choose
   to show that you are now willing to take care of
   yourself.

2) When facing a situation in which you are asked to
   give of yourself this week, ask for some time to get
   back to that person. This will support you to break an
   old pattern of your typical response and practice
   determining how your inner voice is guiding you in
   this situation.

3) Pick anything and enjoy your creative process. Enjoy
   any preparation that needs to go toward your creation

as much as the act of creating itself. It is all creation.
Journal about your creation: what feelings it brings up
in you and if you can acknowledge the beauty in all
you create.

Chapter 3
Fears External to Ourselves

In order to stop struggling and live our life based on the wisdom of our inner voice, we must be willing to address our fears. When our fears are not openly addressed, we hold ourselves back from speaking openly with others, going for our dreams, and sharing who we really are. Many times we are not even aware of how much fear we have and how greatly our fears impact our lives. It is our job to become aware of our fears in order that we will no longer be blocked from living the life we were meant to manifest. Through understanding the different type of fears that we have, we are able to better acknowledge them in order to comprehend the underlying message they provide.

Although we feel all our fears internally, fears can be a result of either internal factors or external factors that we are buying into. We all have fears that are external to ourselves because we recognize that we do not have complete control over our lives. Some examples of external factors include getting laid off from a job, having an accident, going bankrupt, experiencing a natural disaster, or witnessing a terrorist attack. These types of external forces impact our lives, causing us pain. Most of us tend to fear pain and therefore try to do everything in our power trying to avoid it. We can spend a lot of our energy trying to avoid experiences which, in reality, we have little control over. Our fears then gain power over us when we believe in our fears more than we believe in having trust and faith.

Our Perceptions Create Our Reality

Fears are simply false perceptions we have when our attention moves away from our truth. If we examine our fears, they tend to be focused on a sense of lack or loss. Because we have allowed our thoughts to believe that our fears are real, we perceive those types of experiences in our reality. However, when our reality is focused on our inner abundance as well as all that we have been given externally, we will recognize the gifts in our lives.

Of course, remembering our inner abundance can feel challenging when we are faced with shocking news or a dilemma. When some experience strikes my inner core by telling me that myself or my family is not safe or will not have enough, my fear comes up and I react in a panic. I am learning, though, to stop myself in the panic and remember the truth of my internal power.

Our internal power is our core sense of self. From our core, we are able to determine what is right and real for ourselves regardless of how the majority may perceive the circumstances. This is our opportunity to exercise our power, as we define how we view our world. From our core is where I also feel that we are connected to our Divine and able to receive guidance. This guidance is our intuition, gut reaction, or inner voice; it has wisdom to direct us even when we feel afraid.

For me, one of the most challenging areas is remembering my internal sense of power around health issues. In the medical community, doctors deal with the outcome of death and disease. It is their duty, therefore, to warn people when they see that there is potential for physical injury. All of these warnings, however, create an overtone of fear that makes it challenging to listen to and trust our inner voice.

The fears that I see in doctors are only mirroring my own, as a part of me becomes uncertain if I should trust my gut when related to my health issues. It is one thing to trust my gut when ordering a meal at a restaurant and quite another when applying my inner guidance to real-life issues. Yet as we learn that our inner voice will support us every step of the way, we will feel safe trusting the guidance we receive.

In 2001, I developed severe cervical dysplasia, which is a precursor to cervical cancer, and decided to go outside the medical norm for treatment. Rather than going through the typical medical treatment used to treat cervical dysplasia in which a part of my cervix would be cut out, I chose to treat it holistically. Intuitively I felt that having the procedure done could inhibit my ability to conceive, even though there were no studies that suggested implications regarding fertility. My doctor was extremely opposed to my position, warning me of the risks of cancer. She stated, "There is only a slight chance this will heal on its own." However, I did not plan on doing "nothing" as she insinuated. I prayed, visualized, and took supplements. It took nine months, and then the dysplasia was gone. My doctor was in disbelief.

I was happy for two reasons. First, I was happy because the dysplasia was gone! Second, I felt proud of myself because it was the first time I inserted my will to do what felt right to me regarding a major issue in my life. Because I was guided to treat this holistically, I trusted my guidance. It is also important to note that if I had intuitively felt the medical procedure was right for me, that is the route I would have taken. This was not about making a statement; rather, it was about being able to follow the guidance I received without fear. If fear had engulfed me throughout the whole nine months, the outcome would not have turned out as positive.

Now it is 2007 and my cervical dysplasia has come back. Confidently, I felt I could treat it naturally again using the same tools I did back in 2001. To my surprise, the dysplasia has yet to get better.

The dysplasia during this phase of my life has a different message. Instead of inserting my will as the gift as it was in 2001, the message is for me to regain balance in regard to my how I nutritionally feed my body. Again, I am utilizing my internal wisdom to guide me and make substantial changes toward how I choose to fuel my body. Yet I am also aware that the other message is for me to surrender my will this time. If healing does not occur naturally through the nutritional changes I am making, I will gratefully accept the medical treatments in place to help alleviate this condition. Of course, fears still creep in that my condition could worsen, yet I know that my internal guidance is leading me toward a path that will involve healing in many forms. Life is a mystery, and our only challenge is to navigate it through our internal faith.

I look back to a time when my trust in my internal guidance was previously challenged when I became pregnant for the first time. My gut told me to look into having an alternative birth. This was a shock to me, as I always assumed I would get an epidural, since I did not seem to handle pain well. After going to a doctor and not feeling right inside, I checked out midwives. I found the best person I could imagine to support me with my birth and decided a home birth was the route that felt best. Of course, I felt fears, because this was my first child and I had no idea about what giving birth would be like. Yet my inner voice told me this was right, and so I trusted it.

Nevertheless, my fears were mirrored to me through so many people sharing terrible complications such as the umbilical cord being tied, or problems with their baby's heart, or the amount of pain they had giving birth. Despite the stories that depicted peoples' fears, I had the most incredible experience of my life when I gave birth to my daughter in my tub at home. I actually caught her and then I held her in the tub while my husband held me. We were left to bond without disruption, and the connection we made in that moment was indescribable. I have such gratitude for being able to have such a powerful experience to look back upon.

Once I gave birth at home, people told me how brave I was. But my choice was not about bravery or being strong, which would have meant I had made my decision based on my ego. My choice was based on my soul's longing to have the experience of bringing my daughter into the world in a way that felt right to both of us. Through the experience, I did feel powerful as I learned both the strength of my body and Spirit. Yet I believe this is what the process of birth is intended to bring to women in a way they never previously knew. Regardless of how we give birth, it is a powerful experience. Being connected to my inner sense of power allowed me to let go of needing to control how I gave birth and surrender to the process as it was intended.

Facing the Truth that We Do Not Have Control

Most of the experiences in life that cause so much of the fears external to ourselves do so because they are largely out of our control. There is no possible way to protect ourselves from all that could potentially go wrong. However, to admit that we do not have control feels even more frightful. Therefore, we try to alter our behavior or be more alert to all the dangers in the world, hoping we will be protected from something terrible occurring in our lives. Yet internally we know that at any moment, there are numerous ways in which harm could happen to us or those we love.

The tragedy that occurred in the United States on September 11, 2001, is a prime example of how at any moment our lives can be changed in a way we never would have thought possible. The tragedy left some people paralyzed about how they lived because they recognized that they did not have control over their fate and they suffered from Post Traumatic Stress Disorder, or PTSD. Because of this trauma, the way all of us think, perceive, and feel has been altered to a certain degree. When people experience PTSD, it is because their beliefs about life have been dramatically impacted.

After September 11, our awareness was heightened by the fact that in an instant, our lives could be completely changed or no longer exist. The fear instilled in us was exactly the outcome that the terrorists hoped to induce. The terrorists knew from their own experiences that when we react through our fear and hatred, we will not be able to truly own our strength. Fear brings forth reactionary behavior, which inhibits our power. That was the goal of the terrorists.

What we must consider is that when we are taking action based on our sense of fear, we create more fear in our lives. Due to our heightened fears about life, we may attempt to cover ourselves every way possible to keep us safe. This is true whether we are talking about riding a bike or if we are trying to secure our nation against another terrorist attack. Of course, deep down we know that it is impossible to always stay safe from harm. When we are focused on how to prevent being harmed, we are living in a reactionary way. When we are reactionary, our focus on fear creates more fearful experiences, which leaks our power and energy away from being able to create the life we desire. However, if we decide to live proactively by focusing on what we would like to create in our lives, we create more of those experiences and feel powerful being able to create change.

There are numerous examples I could give to demonstrate this principle. What comes to mind is one of the issues I had with my children. Beginning at age two, my twin sons were constantly fighting and setting each other off. This, of course, caused chaos in our house and made my job much more hectic. I was worn out by their behavior. I focused on how I could prevent them from fighting and what more I could do with my parenting skills to improve the situation. I was focused on my fear of their fighting, which disrupted me and our home.

After a few weeks of trying everything under the sun with my kids, such as time-outs, giving them time apart from one another, and occasional yelling, I remembered how focusing on what I do not desire will create more of what I do not want. I chose to change my focus toward the experiences I would like to have with my children and how grateful I felt

that I have this time with them. The next morning, I visualized the day we would have together and how I would feel. I
saw my children and me playing with each other and having
fun. If an issue came up, I would be able to shift their energy
back to a harmonic state with ease. To my amazement, the
fighting was dramatically reduced. When it did occur, I was
able to move past it much more easily because I was no
longer focused on it. Because my focus was on what I
desired, in an instant I would come up with something that
would switch the energy to having more fun or cooperation.
With my frame of mind being on having fun, I was led to
turning on music or using a silly voice to make a shift in our
environment, rather than the voice of exhaustion that used to
overcome me.

Think of the experiences that we go over and over in our
mind. We tend to do this with what we do not desire to have
in our lives. Whether it is going on another bad date, getting
another bill that we feel challenged to pay, or dealing with an
undesirable coworker, our focus stays on what we are
dreading. What are we gaining from doing this? As we have
likely found, we get more of the same type of experiences.
What we lose is more significant as we waste energy that
could have been going toward creating our desired experiences rather than reiterating those we do not want.

Because our mind is so powerful, thinking about how we
may get harmed opens the door to experiencing pain in our
lives. If we believe we will likely get harmed, we will have
experiences that demonstrate or mirror this belief to us. We
create a reality that matches our perceptions in order to feel
justified and right in our beliefs. Thus, our thinking of fear
creates more of the experiences we do not desire, which
depletes our energy to create what we do want in life.

Think about when we are learning something new. If our
focus is on how we do not want to mess up, or physically hurt
ourselves, we will not do as well. If we are open to the
learning process and see how others have been able to do

what we are learning, we will feel more confident about succeeding.

Look back at learning to ride a bike. If our focus is on the ground because that is where we think we are going to fall, we cannot look up and see where we are going. We need to be able to trust that regardless what happens, we can pick ourselves up and be all right. Otherwise we will struggle with obtaining our desires.

One man who is in sales shared with me his fear about a current deal that he had going on at work. He needed this deal to close, or he would be struggling financially. In his recent past, he'd had deals that suddenly went sour. Without having the income from those other deals, he felt even more pressure to have this current deal close. His fear was not having enough money to provide for his family.

With this current deal, there were reasons that made him believe it was against the odds that it would close. I reminded him that if his focus remained on the logical issues as to why the deal would not close, he would likely create that exact experience. I suggested for him to focus on the outcome he desired and trust that the money he needed would come into his life. A month later, the deal closed despite the logical reasons he feared.

After discussing his experience, I asked him what was different for him between the situations when the deals blew up and the one that closed. There were two differences. First, he learned that it did not support him to focus on the outcome he did not want. Second, he recognized that in those deals that went sour, he felt in his gut that something was not right with the other parties involved, as there were aspects about them he did not trust. Thus, he was able to recognize the difference between the information his mind gave him, which was the logical rationale, versus his gut, which was accurate.

Trust in Our Intuition Rather Than Logic Alone

How do we begin changing our thoughts so we are not paralyzed by our fear? In order to be able to shift our thoughts, we need to begin listening more and more to our inner voice, or gut, which is our intuition. Our rational mind, which tends to control our thoughts, wants understanding and to be able to predict how events will unfold. This limits our mind from perceiving different possibilities. Our inner voice, on the other hand, is open to endless possibilities. Our inner voice is connected to our Source, in which anything is possible and thus defies logic. Learning to connect to our intuition will allow us to alleviate our fears, as we follow our inner voice and experience events that go against logic.

Through learning to let go of my logic and listen to my inner voice, I have experienced over and over how much more aligned my experiences are with my heart's desires. I compare this to when in the past I would have allowed my logic to steer me and I would end up feeling somehow limited or unsatisfied. One common experience I previously had was not speaking up around others, especially those I did not know. I would hesitate because I would try to figure out how each person might react to what I would have to say. Before I knew it, the moment would be gone and I would be left with a sense of disappointment for not offering what I wanted to share.

Having enough experiences in which I felt disappointed because I did not listen to my inner voice is what allowed me to begin following my intuitive guidance. The more I did, the more comfortable I became. I also gained confidence in myself, which supported me not to listen to others' reactions to my decisions when I am following my gut. I know that although my decisions may appear to others to be poor ones, they are right for me and thus always work out as such. Nevertheless, I still have moments when my fears take over and I question following my inner guidance.

One of those moments happened not too long ago as I was discussing an event that happened earlier in my day. That morning, I went grocery shopping with my three kids. I left the side door of my minivan open while I was buckling each of them into their car seats. I was startled when suddenly a man started speaking to my kids. I looked up and his head was in the door. Fortunately, I saw that the man was at least eighty, and I felt that even though the situation was a bit odd, we were safe.

What brought up my sense of fear about the experience was that my gut reaction was questioned. In the evening when I shared the harmless experience at the grocery store with my husband, he became very concerned. He did not care that the man was elderly. He did not think it was safe.

I do not blame my husband for feeling that way, as there are people who cause others harm. His reaction, however, set off the fear within me. My fear triggered thoughts, such as the elderly man possibly being a ploy, while someone else could have jumped in the front seat. This is just one of numerous scenarios the fear played out in my head.

When I followed and trusted my gut at the time of the experience, none of those fearful scenarios came to my mind. Because I trusted my inner voice, I knew I was in alignment with my heart and the experiences it desires for me to have. In doing so, I felt that I was okay. My husband's reaction to the situation triggered my mind to take over, which filled me with fear. When I buy into fear is when I begin questioning myself, because I am then cutting off my connection with my Source.

My fear takes over when it tells me that if that scenario had gone badly, I would have felt helpless. When we feel like there is nothing we can do, when we have no control over a situation, we feel vulnerable and our fear kicks into high gear. We become paralyzed by our fear because we are cutting ourselves off from our Source. Thus, the true meaning of fear is when we are separated from our connection to our Source and ignore our inner guidance.

The reality is there was nothing to question. If the situation was unsafe, my intuition would have told me before the man got close to my car. My intuition would have led me to see him out of the corner of my eye, telling me to close and lock the door. Or my inner voice would have guided me to know exactly what to do to get out of the unsafe situation.

Why Bad Things Happen to People

Explaining why painful events happen in our lives can feel controversial to many because we label painful experiences as bad. We label pain as bad because if we had a choice, logically we would rather not have hurtful experiences to contend with. However, it is our limited understanding that labels events as bad simply because they cause us pain. From a spiritual perspective, we recognize that all situations occur in order for us to grow and become more aligned with our heart's desire. Our Spirit wants us to become all that we are meant to become in this lifetime. In order for that to happen, we have to go through experiences that lead to our growth and that force us to change.

When we willingly follow our intuition, we create changes in our life that go against what we would consider our typical or logical reaction. When we do not listen to our inner voice, however, the Universe needs to create scenarios in order to make shifts for us to become more aligned with our inner truth. We then may experience something we call "bad" because it creates pain. However, pain can be a great gift because it forces us to make changes that we have been unwilling to do.

Many people may likely get upset reading this, because then they look at painful situations that have happened to them and become angry that I am suggesting that they look at those experiences as a gift. First of all, when we first experience a traumatic event, we should grieve or experience whatever feelings are authentically coming from inside. In order to work through our pain, we must allow ourselves to express our pain authentically.

Working through our traumatic experiences can be very challenging to actually do. Trauma takes over us in the way we think, what we do, and how we dream. It is life changing, which is the point. Did we choose to have any of those horrific things happen to us, whether it was being raped, being abandoned, losing a child, witnessing genocide, or anything else? Of course no one would ever choose trauma or pain. However, from a spiritual perspective, even though we do not like the pain, we recognize pain as a tool that is intended to move us in the direction we ultimately desire.

Learning to Let Go of Our Pain

When we feel harmed by an experience, we must allow ourselves to feel the pain that is within us. We should never deny our feelings because they are authentic to our truth. Our Spirit needs us to openly express all of the anger, hurt, frustration, and sense of hopelessness within ourselves from being harmed. If we deny that those feelings are present within us, we will have an even greater sense of being victimized, as we are not allowing ourselves to speak and feel our truth.

When we feel badly hurt, sharing our emotions, thoughts, and feelings with others whom we trust and who listen to us is essential. This is where therapy can be very supportive, as there is something healing about having someone serve as a witness to our pain. Having our pain validated by another helps us to move forward by creating the time and space for us to recognize our true feelings. Going through this process gives us a greater understanding of how we were allowing our pain to run our lives. Living our lives that way is so much more limiting. Being able to free ourselves from those shackles allows us to carry on with creating the life we desire.

We Must Let Go of Being the Victim in Order to Own Our Power

Part of the lesson for all of us who have been hurt is to no longer play the victim and instead claim our power. It is always challenging to overcome feeling victimized, because there is justification for how a victim feels. However, after the point comes when the person who has been harmed has shared, expressed, and mourned all of her feelings (which may take years), she has to make a choice. She can continue to express her feelings and hope someday that those who have caused her harm will admit to their wrongdoings. The other, more empowering, choice is to let go of the pain.

Anyone who considers her or himself a victim of being harmed by another needs to ask, "Who does it serve more by me remaining bitter, hurt, and sad?" The answer is that *it always hurts ourselves more and actually benefits those who caused us pain*. How does our pain serve those who caused it? Because when we remain the victim, we are never able to claim our power. How can we? We are the victim, and victims do not have power. Therefore, those in power will continue to control those who claim themselves as victims. Change will not occur until we say to ourselves, "No more will I stay being a victim as a benefit for those who have hurt me."

In order to let go of being the victim, we need to let go and even forgive those who have caused us pain. In forgiving, we are not letting our abusers off the hook. Instead, we are simply becoming wise enough to understand that holding on to someone hurting us only harms ourselves.

I remember being freed from the painful experiences in my past once I realized it was unlikely that I would ever get an apology or even an admission of wrongdoing from those who hurt me. Furthermore, I recognized I could never force an apology to happen. I can try many tactics, but the truth is that those who have hurt me do not have to recognize the pain they have caused me. They will never see the experiences that impacted me exactly the way I do and therefore may find no need to admit that they were wrong. Once I recognized I could point a gun to their head and nothing would really change from them, I realized what a waste of my precious time it was in desiring them to admit their wrongdoings. Even if I pointed a gun to their head, they might say they were wrong out of fear, but they might not necessarily feel wrong. What I really desired was for them to **know** they were wrong.

I realized, however, that in wanting something from those who had harmed me (i.e., an apology), I was still allowing them to control me. That really pissed me off! I am still allowing them to control me? Yes! In wanting them to say sorry to me or acknowledge their wrongdoings, my energy is being wasted on them instead of me.

Being able to recognize how I was still permitting those to hurt me by wanting an apology allowed me to let go of that need. I had to; otherwise I felt like I would be banging my head against a wall for the rest of my life. So I let go, not for them but for me. I was holding myself captive by the hurt they caused. My only choice left was to choose differently. I could stay paralyzed being the victim, desperately needing an apology to make myself feel better, or I could work on getting myself to feel better without needing anything from those who caused me harm.

The Lessons Gained from Our Pain

I have learned to give thanks for my pain. Why? Not because I desired the pain I went through but because it hurt me enough so I would have to change. Again, that pain was necessary in order for me to gain the strength to be the person I need to be in order for me to do my life's work. Without being the victim, I would not have felt that inner force that said **"No More Will I Be Willing to Be the Victim! I Will Take Responsibility Now to Own My Power!"**

The gift in being the victim is this: we eventually become tired of it which, allows us to become willing to own and take responsibility for our power. Think about it. It is so much easier to be the victim. When we are the victim, nothing is our fault. The fault is our abusers'. It is much easier to say that our life sucks or is not how we desire it to be because of someone else.

It takes much more time, energy, willingness, and love for ourselves to say, "My life is not how I desire it to be, and I have the power to change that regardless of what others do or do not think of me. I am now willing to give myself the gift of what I once believed others have taken from me. I recognize that they are not that powerful to actually take anything away from me unless I allow it."

As I am able to look back on those experiences, the reason I felt sad and a victim was because I was a victim of myself. My Spirit wanted me to know my truth, and when I bought into being the victim, I could not possibly own my power or magnificence. When I bought into being the victim, I felt they took something from me because they caused me pain. So I chose to no longer give them that power. Instead, I gave to myself anything that I felt they had taken from me. I gave it to myself with love, because I knew that was the reason my Spirit was crying out to me. My Spirit was creating this sadness because as the victim, I refused to treat myself with love.

As I finally gave myself the love I deeply desired, I felt sadness for those who had caused me pain. I knew that those who hurt me must also carry pain within themselves. I recognized that I was now moving beyond my pain toward loving, honoring, and nurturing myself. Those who had hurt me, on the other hand, were still stuck living in fear.

When we are on our way to creating the life we truly desire, know that those who have abused others are lost in their pain, which causes them to hurt or manipulate others. They abuse because they still rely on others to meet their needs. We, on the other hand, have the wisdom to recognize that we are the only ones who can truly fulfill our inner needs. Because we are now on the path to learn to care for our inner needs, we are becoming filled with passion, inspiration, and purpose. Those who abuse, however, remain struggling with their emptiness, hatred, or sense of lack. Because we are willing to take back our power, our life is filled with abundance where we once perceived lack.

If trying to comprehend the rationale behind those who caused you harm just feels like buying into an excuse, then know that you are still in pain. This is okay, because wherever you are now is perfect for you at this time. I must emphasize the importance of embracing your feelings as they are in the present moment. Otherwise you will not be able to move forward. By continuing to address your feelings, you will come to a point when you authentically decide for yourself whether or not you are willing to live with or without the pain.

It is important to recognize that often we choose pain. Why? Because that is what we know, that is what we are familiar with, and it feels safer. It is only when we have had enough of the pain and how it runs our lives that we will choose otherwise. In other words, it is only when we are so damn tired of the pain that we will be willing to do whatever it takes to make changes in our lives. Being sick and tired of the pain gives us enough gumption to take the necessary risks entailed with us owning our full power.

How Our Fears Support Us

Our fears are present in our lives to move us past our ego. We experience fears when we are disconnected from our truth. Our fears continue to escalate until we are willing to let go of the control our ego has over us, which is preventing us from seeing our truth. When we come from our truth, we recognize that there is nothing to fear, because we are always being taken care of by the Universe. In other words, we need to get to the point where we say to ourselves, "Who cares? If my fear happens, I do not have control over it anyway." After we are able to address our fear, we are able to know the truth of how powerful we actually are.

Many of my clients have expressed not liking to have to confront people, as they fear making them upset. When an issue comes up that they know does not sit well with them, they become filled with worry trying to determine what to say, or whether to say anything. Some get physically sick, as their stomach tosses and turns over the issue. Others lose sleep.

When my clients share with me physical symptoms, most often it is because they have not been willing to address how they are feeling. When any of us feels physically sick when preoccupied with an emotional issue, our bodies are trying to tell us that something is not right for us. If we choose not to address the issue, we will continue to not feel well. Once we express ourselves, however, we will find that our symptoms go away.

It is important to note that when we address how we are feeling, we will get a different outcome than if we try to confront our fears without connecting to our emotions. When we share our feelings, we are opening ourselves up, which allows us to connect with others. Even if that connection becomes challenging, we are coming from our truth and not our ego.

Confronting our fears, on the other hand, makes us try to create an image of ourselves that is likely not aligned with our truth. This is when our egos come forth, because we are envisioning the experience to be difficult, and we feel we must put forth our emotional protective armor, which is our ego. Utilizing our ego creates more strain, because there is a lack of real connection when we are putting up false pretenses. Without coming from our truth, we will have a harder time finding a resolution that feels right.

When my clients first begin to share their truth, often times they are also sharing their ego. This is normal, because most of us feel vulnerable sharing our emotions. Because of their vulnerability, they feel they must carry that protective armor. Therefore, in reality they are only partially expressing themselves. Often times they become more willing to share that they are angry than the more vulnerable feeling of being sad. Although sharing their anger is a great step toward being authentic, truly being open with their emotions would allow them to share how they are hurt and sad. When they allow themselves to be truly open and let go of their ego, they always find the resolution they desire.

We also have to address their fears of not wanting to hurt anyone. They share a common illusion, which is that we have control over how people will react to us. This is when we must check in with ourselves and ask what feelings are really behind the fear of not wanting to hurt others. In most circumstances, the fear is an internal fear of not being accepted or liked if we are to share our truth.

When my clients become willing to address aspects of their life that are not working well for them, I ask them how they feel afterward. Most commonly they feel a little anxiety, as a part of them worries how the other people involved perceived them. When asked to check in with their core sense of self, however, they always share either happiness or pride for being able to come forward with sharing how they truly felt. They inwardly sense that they are becoming more able to own their truth and therefore their power. The more they practice, the easier it becomes for them to claim and create their ideal life.

Examples of Turning Pain into Personal Power

History demonstrates to us that many of the people who have made the greatest strides to advance our human development are people who were able to utilize their pain in order to create change. Regardless of the degree of harm that occurred, there have been people who have been able to reclaim their voice. By acknowledging how the pain impacted them and allowing their Spirit to guide them, they were able to make desperately needed changes.

The Rev. Dr. Martin Luther King, Jr., is a great example of a person who made a major impact on race relations in the United States due to the mistreatment he experienced because he was African American. Dr. King was able to inspire and move people to listen to their inner knowing and Spirit. He did not buy into the belief that he was a victim, even though he had been caused pain by many. That was not his mentality. Rather, it was through a love for himself and others that he felt passion for speaking his truth. Because Dr. King did not have a sense of anger in his heart, he was able to speak his truth through compassion and conviction for his beliefs. Coming from a place in which he valued all humankind, he was able to touch so many, and they listened.

Through his own ability to claim his power, because no one was going to hand it to him, he was able to create major shifts in our society. He knew this power was not something to be given to him by others, especially by those who used their power to try to control him. This power is within each of us and is simply waiting for us to know ourselves enough to claim it.

There are countless others such as Gandhi, St. Joan of Arc, Elizabeth Cady Stanton, and Nelson Mandela, just to name a few. All of these people claimed their personal power in order to create necessary changes. Because of their example, we were taught the strength of utilizing peaceful methods to stand in our truth. We were also taught how one person can begin to manifest change by creating unity among thousands.

None of the aforementioned people was full of hatred. If so, they could not have touched so many and created the change they did because the dynamics would have been different. They would have been in some way asking or demanding justice instead of claiming it through their truth as they did. They stood lovingly and strongly in their truth, which allowed them to claim their power.

There is a subtle difference between claiming and demanding. These people did not buy into being a victim because they knew their power regardless of whether others wanted to recognize it or not. They utilized their personal sense of power in order to ignite this power within others as well. Through coming from a place of inner power, they had no need to try to demand justice. Rather, they claimed justice by simply being in their truth and speaking from that place.

When we buy into that we are unequal, we do not treat those who oppose us with respect. We are in essence putting ourselves in a one-down position, in which we feel we must fight to be heard, understood, or recognized. If we see ourselves in a one-down position, then, of course, those to whom we are giving away our power will remain having power over us. Again, it is our view of ourselves, in which we make ourselves the victim, that creates a cycle in which we are unable to own our power.

When we know our worth, we give others respect regardless of their views. As we give others respect, we claim respect for ourselves. Treating others with disrespect comes from the same fear and sense of lack that created the injustice or abuse in the first place. Being respectful toward others and demonstrating human dignity comes from love within oneself. Having that sense of knowingness about our truth and worth is unstoppable.

Even with death, the lessons and models these people demonstrated carry on within us. Still today, we recognize that what these leaders shared was pure truth from Spirit that instilled change within countries and within our hearts. What is important to remember is that these people chose to share their voice regardless of what others thought of them. Even if at times they were afraid to speak their truth, they did so because they knew within themselves the consequences of their choice. If they had chosen to not share their truth, we would all have suffered. Thankfully, they believed in their truth enough to speak it loud and clear to all those around them.

On a personal level, we must each be able to do this in order to claim the life we desire. We have to be willing to express what is acceptable to us and what we will not tolerate. Hence, when we choose to know our truth, we become a model for others to know that it is possible for them to do the same, regardless of whether we are famous or not.

It is the intention of the Universe for each of us to know love and a sense of honor within ourselves. When we do not know this, we create a lot of pain in our lives. We need to be willing to take responsibility to truly own our power and utilize our inner strength to do what is right for ourselves personally, in our communities, and throughout the world. Otherwise, drama and violence will continue in our lives until we become willing. The question is how far will violence and fear within our hearts or society have to escalate until we become willing to act?

Putting this Chapter into Practice:
1) Recall experiences in your past in which you used your gut reaction to make a decision. Utilize these experiences to support you into accepting how your gut has and will continue to support you.
2) Name any of the fears that you worry about. How does your inner voice or gut view the situation that you fear? Is there a way to change your perspective that feels more empowering *and* is believable to your rationale mind?
3) Can you look at your past experiences and think of an incident that still brings you pain? Examine your own process and determine if you have not fully grieved the incident, feel like the victim, or are numbed by the experience. If you were forced to share one way that you have learned or even gained from the incident,

what would that be? Journal your reactions, thoughts, and feelings.

Chapter 4
Addressing Our Internal Fears

Addressing the fears that are external to us is a crucial component of living a balanced, peaceful, and joyful life. Another component we must also recognize are the fears within us that are about ourselves. As mentioned in Chapter 3, fears are misperceptions, and most of us have plenty of misperceptions about ourselves. Our misperceptions again are based on a sense of lack, yet this time the belief is about us. We have bought into believing that who we are is somehow bad or not enough and lacks worth or value. When we view ourselves with this type of negativity, once more we are buying into fears that are based upon our ego.

The Purpose and Development of Our Ego

When we were young, most of us found out it was not safe to always be who we truly are because we were put down for it or ridiculed. Through the miraculous nature of our humanness, we were designed with a mechanism to protect our Spirit, or our true self, when we did not have the ability to do so on our own. This mechanism is the ego. Due to the deep pain many of us went through when our Spirit felt rejected by others who were important to us, we learned to push down our true self, and our ego helped us hide.

Our egos become a part of our lives in order for us to cope, especially when we are young and adjusting to this human experience. What we are adjusting to is the human experience of love, which is different than the unconditional love in the Spirit realm. We are so hurt in our core for no longer experiencing this unconditional love that we need our egos to protect us from further emotional/spiritual injury. We need this while we are young and learning the conditions of our human environment; otherwise, we would feel too much pain to survive.

In our youth, we do not have many other options but to take the experiences we are given. Our egos form to protect our Spirit from the conditions we go through that are not for our highest good. Having our ego actually helps support our young Spirit to adjust to not receiving love simply based on our essence. As a part of our emotional and spiritual survival, we learn to hide our truth and change ourselves in order to receive the conditional love that is the norm of the human experience. Through our ego, we create a false self that knows how to receive the love or attention we desire. This is how our egos develop and then have the potential to take over our sense of who we are.

At some point, it is our job to recognize when we are able to stand up for ourselves and our truth, and no longer have to rely on the false pretenses of the ego. If we continue to allow the ego to run our lives, we lose who we are. We forget what brings joy, passion, and laughter to our lives. Since we lost what fulfills us, we look for things outside ourselves to try to fill the void that we feel from being so disconnected from our truth. We use alcohol, drugs, shopping, gambling, sex, food, and video games as well as numerous other ways to try to avoid remembering the pain we are in because we, too, have rejected our inner voice. We are so lost from knowing who we are because we, too, have bought into the lie that who we truly are is of no or little good.

For this reason, some spiritual teachers have told us it is our job to banish the ego from our lives and our hearts. The real issue that has been missing is the purpose of the ego. Once we understand that the ego has been in our lives to support us, we do not have to try so hard to reject this part of ourselves. It is simply our job to determine when we feel we are ready to truly be in our truth in order that we can rely less on our ego to protect us. In the meantime, we can give thanks that the ego formed when it did, because it was the only mechanism we had to help us cope, to endure the pain of being rejected as we were.

In our youth, we could not comprehend the reasons why we were being rejected. The ego formed knowing it should protect this precious, unique, and beautiful you. The ego, like everything else created within us, has its purpose. Thanks to the development of the ego, our Spirit could not be taken away completely. Our ego had to do a superior job of protecting our true self because the alternative is not a good option. We all know what happens to people when their Spirit is broken. They give up and then they die. Our ego prevented us from giving up on our life.

I now thank my ego for protecting me when it did. It did a great job. However, now I am older. I am able to recognize how I have allowed my internal fears to run my life. I am in a position now to make choices for myself. The key for myself has been recognizing when the ego is no longer serving me and to move forward. Then I am able to say thank you and let go.

The Ego's Fight

When we first confront our internal fears, the ego puts up a fight, because the ego's job is to protect us. Our ego will therefore push back when we say to our ego we are okay without it. We may be saying to ourselves that we are able to let our truth come forward no matter what others think. The ego is smart and a gift, because if we just said "Thanks, ego, but I no longer need you," and began to show our true selves, we would likely get hurt. Our ego knows not to trust us without us being able to demonstrate that we believe in our truth. The ego will bring up our fears because it needs to be certain that we no longer need the same degree of protection.

The Universe in all its wisdom continues to give us experiences that allow us to challenge our fears. As we confront our fears, we are tested to see how our fears will impact our feelings, thoughts, and behaviors. Through each instance of fear that we choose not to allow to impact our sense of self, we demonstrate that we are able to let go of our ego's protection to a certain degree. The more we give up our ego's protection, the further we will be challenged in order to live life in our truth. Bit by bit, through each experience, as we confront our fears, we get back our inner voice. As we do, we are able to recognize for ourselves that buying into the fear and being someone we are not no longer serves us. Eventually it is our inner voice that is more prominent than our fears or our ego's voice.

I like to look at ourselves as an onion. We continue to peel away the layers of falseness that have formed around our core, true selves. Just as with peeling a real onion, as we peel away these layers of falseness and fear, tears are often involved. Each layer of falseness removed gets us closer to living more completely from our truth, from our core, as we no longer buy into that layer of lies. Through this experience of removing one layer at a time, we are able to recognize our inner voice more clearly each time. We are also able to recognize that the fear we are currently experiencing is present because we are in the process of stepping further into our truth and letting ourselves shine.

Shedding the Layers of my Fear

Learning to understand the voice of my fear has been a work in progress. Fear used to control me and to some degree still does. Fear does not, however, run my life like it used to do. Not too many years ago, fear was the prominent voice in my head, which made me a completely different person. As I mentioned in Chapter 1, I was convinced that if I were to show who I really was, I would not be loved or even liked. Because I bought into my fears that I was a bad person who never measured up, I attempted in all my efforts to be the type of person everyone would like. I wanted and desperately tried to be perfect in every way. In doing so, I had no clue about the truth of who I was. My inner voice was deeply pushed down and buried, to the extent that it was nearly impossible for me to pay attention to my Spirit or my inner voice.

At this point in my life, I now feel fortunate that I have had a lot of experience in dealing with my fears. As I begin a new phase of expressing myself and my truth, my ego is here yet again, making sure I am ready to take this next step. There have been times in writing this book that my fears have come to try to take over me with such force. My fears of not being good enough or having any worth try to seep in and diminish me, but my experiences have allowed me to recognize those thoughts as my fears. I have heard those thoughts over and over in my life, especially when I am attempting something new. By learning to address them in a supportive manner, experience by experience, I recognize that they are not the truth.

My fears, if I listen to the message behind what I am being told, can actually guide me back to my truth. What I have found is that my fears are demonstrating to me my propensity to turn outside of myself for approval. When I go back to this habit that is not for my highest good, my fears kick into high gear. By understanding my fears, I see that fear is alerting me that I am straying from my truth. My Spirit knows my truth and guides me accordingly. My choice is to determine which path I want to continue to follow. Fortunately, I have found that the path of fear is much less fun than the voice of my Spirit.

The gift of working with my fears is that their effect on me is less and less because I know my truth more and more. On challenging days, I buy into my fears for a few hours. Typically, if they come up, I entertain them for a moment and then let them go. Even though my inner voice gets clouded at times because of my fears, I have learned through the past that this is just another ego test. If I want change, I know what to do. I know enough to listen to my inner voice, because then I get to experience the truth of who I am. By allowing myself to live in truth, I experience true joy and passion for living. Living life in this way makes continuing to confront my fears worth doing!

Utilizing Our Life as Our Mirror

Becoming aware of how our lives are impacted by our fears can be challenging. Many times we may not even be aware that we have any fears. Our fears are impacting us when our lives are not going in the direction we desire, yet we cannot figure out why that is. The reason we cannot figure this out is because our ego is protecting us from our fears by keeping them at an unconscious level. Since the fears are not in our awareness, we cannot pinpoint why our lives are not going as we would like.

One tool that can support us to recognize our unconscious fears is viewing our life as a mirror. Viewing our life as a mirror allows us to see how the people and events in our life are reflecting back to us our inner world. Sometimes we can easily notice this with our best friend, when she seems to be going through a similar challenge even though her circumstances are completely different from our own. In those instances, we are more open to seeing the similarity, or the mirror, because we like and respect our best friend.

What is challenging is to see is our life as a mirror in *all* of our experiences, especially those with which we feel the most challenged. Know that when we feel a strong emotional pull or struggle with another, whether it is our boss, relative, spouse, or child, our inner world is being reflected to us. By allowing ourselves to step back, we can experience for ourselves how our life is really reflecting our perspective of ourselves.

One example that was really helpful for me to experience and observe was going with my daughter Avery to her first day of preschool. Watching her that day demonstrated to me how she is mirroring my own life, as to how I am handling entering into a new situation with my career. Avery felt very anxious as her first day of school began to approach. She knew that school meant that she would be without her Mommy, who represented safety, love, and comfort. Even though going to school could also mean more freedom for her, greater exploration, and more friends, she could not focus on those positive aspects, as she had yet to experience them. Even though a part of her was extremely excited about going to school, the closer the first day came, the more scared she became. All she was focusing on was what she felt, which was how hard it would be for her to let go and know that she would be okay without the familiarity and comfort of her mom being by her side.

It brings tears to my eyes just writing about it, as it did on her first day of school when she cried and begged for me not to leave her. She touched me, because I could so easily relate to her feelings of fear and clutching onto her present life, not wanting it to change. At the same time, I knew within me that she was ready for the change. She wanted to feel more independent and demonstrate that she could do things on her own. In other words, she wanted to experience more of her internal power. She felt so much pride that first morning putting on her backpack, which made her feel like a big girl.

Her experience was such a mirror to my own life at the time. The emotions, the fears she experienced from her own change in life reflected mine as well, as I was creating change in my life through my career. Although I desired for this change to occur, I was fighting it as well. Just as I had to persuade Avery on her first day of school to even go through the schoolyard gate, it also pained me at times to take the necessary steps to make my desires my reality. After getting her through the gate, I again had to coax her into going through the door of her classroom building, and then her classroom, because she recognized what that step meant for her.

Just like Avery, at times, I could only focus on the loss I was experiencing. I was apprehensive about writing or taking action toward my career because I was so afraid. After all, my life was very comfortable. My life as it was felt safe and full of love. I knew I was already very blessed. However, I also recognized that there was a part of me not yet expressed that deeply desired to be. If I played it safe and did not coax and persuade myself against all my fears to move forward, then I knew my desires could never happen.

Avery also demonstrated to me that even though she was excited about the prospect of going to school, the change also made her feel apprehensive about her future. Even when we know the future holds for us amazing experiences, we can be scared to step forward. After seeing Avery's apprehension, I was able to admit to myself my own sense of doubt about the potential of my career. "What would my life be like if my desires regarding my career came true? Would I feel over-whelmed, stressed, and imbalanced?" I wondered. My reflection of this experience allowed me to recognize the gift, which is knowing that when my fear questions my desires, it is my ego at work. My ego is testing me to see if I am ready to shine brightly as I live from my truth.

By seeing the mirror of my daughter's process as she entered a new phase of her life, I was able to recognize my own fears more easily. Seeing how I helped her demonstrated how to give myself the support I need as well. Just as with Avery–having to support her to work through her fears of first entering the gate, then the building, then the classroom door, and finally letting me leave–I realized I had to do the same for myself.

I will continue to have stages of fear in my personal and professional development; the difference is I will l have no one physically present to support me to move forward. If I do not allow myself to take these steps, no one will. In being able to take a step back from life and see the parallel process we were going through, I became more aware of my fears. Being aware allowed me to take the lead in addressing blocks that would inhibit me living the life I desire.

Our Perceptions of Others Reflects Our Inner Truth

Another tool that helps us recognize our blocks is by noticing our perceptions of others. Examining those perceptions depicts an accurate reflection of our inner world. We can only see within others what we know. Naturally our attention goes toward what we focus on in life. Therefore, depending upon what our inner focus is, that is what we will be drawn to recognizing in others.

Allowing ourselves to recognize our perceptions of others in this way can support us toward becoming more aware of our inner process. For instance, if we are constantly being critical of others, we should know that internally we are even harsher toward ourselves. Many times it is challenging for us to recognize that we are actually having these feelings internally. Because it may be difficult for us to own certain aspects of ourselves, we shift our attention toward others. At times, we may project our feelings, which means we are making up in our own mind aspects about another that are not present because the attributes come from ourselves.

Energetically we all feel how we are being perceived. We either feel at ease or uncomfortable because of the other person's vibe. Our vibe is a reflection of our inner world. Depending on whether we are feeling good or bad about ourselves, we will give off a different vibe. Therefore, when we perceive ourselves in a critical manner, we will tend to look for the same in others. People sense our negativity about ourselves, others, and life.

When we think about it, when we are feeling down, we typically do not give out compliments. When we are in a good mood and feeling peace within, we see and share with others the good we see in them. Again, we can only see within others what we see within ourselves.

Being able to recognize our emotional states as well as identifying others' vibes will be extremely helpful in being able to create and maintain the energy state we desire. In order to do that, we must become aware of how we perceive others. Are we judging them in some form or fashion right away? If so, what are the judgments about? Hence, knowing that we are judging others can support us to address our critical voice and allow us to discover the need we are serving when we choose critical behavior.

As I was able to recognize how constantly I was judging others, I began to understand how harsh I was being toward myself. It pained me to admit that I was so critical toward others because deep down I knew I was a good person. I did not feel like a good person, though, because I was so judgmental. My reason for judging was because I had a very critical voice within me watching every action I took. Through the eyes of my inner critic, there was no room to be human. I was tortured with never feeling "good enough," and therefore I never saw others as "good enough" either. In an instant, I could see what was "wrong" with someone else, because that was how often I judged myself, instant by instant.

During that time in my life, the Law of Attraction was working against me because I was working against myself. The Law of Attraction states that like attracts like. Because I had a negative perception of myself, I attracted others in my life who felt the same toward themselves and others. Together we would try convincing ourselves that there was nothing wrong with us, as we concluded it was everyone else who was not right in some way. Our negative energy attracted more negative energy, which was why I experienced many dramas during that time in my life. My negativity about myself was a magnet for bad things happening to me.

Of course, I did not recognize how my thoughts and feelings about myself were attracting what I did not want in my life. For this reason, it is imperative for us to become aware of our thoughts, feelings, and fears. Otherwise we will continue to bring into our lives experiences and people that are the opposite of what we desire.

The good news is that all the harshness and pain I brought into my life occurred in order that I might turn back to remembering my truth. Once I realized how unhappy I truly was, I reached out for support and began therapy. Having an outside perspective from the typical bad energy I attracted allowed the critical veil to lift in order that I could see reality through a more gentle perspective. As I became more tolerant of myself, I was more tolerant of others. My perspective changed from being critical of others to noticing the goodness from within people.

At the same time, I found mentors in alternative healing modalities and learned the impact our energy has on one another. I learned to become less tolerant of negative energy. This was a time in which I felt I had to let go of friends who wanted to remain caught up in negative vibes. Letting go of people in our lives who are caught in negative energy is imperative to our overall health. Negative energy is toxic for our emotional, spiritual, and physical health.

As we move from getting rid of our toxic energy, we will naturally shift toward wanting more loving energy surrounding us. Again, like attracts like, and as our internal perspective shifts, we become open to drawing people and situations that are aligned with our desires. The more we are aligned with our truth, the more in sync we will be with attracting our desires.

Having uplifting, loving energy to support us will help us sustain the energy we desire to maintain even when our energy shifts back to an imbalanced state. Rather than having others who are in pain trying to offer us more fear-filled views of life, we will have loving energy to help remind us that who we are from within is our truth. As we begin to see how fortunate we are to have the people and experiences that we have, we know this is a reflection of our inner state. Seeing what we are capable of achieving when we are willing to address our fears demonstrates that the more we are willing to own our truth, the more our reality will reflect our desires. Our ego and fears support us to find our truth when we become willing to honor all of who we are.

Others' Reactions to Fear

When we admit that we are afraid, we are going to be better served by those who can support us to listen to our truth. Currently there has been so much said to people about "breaking through their fears" that people feel the need to fight themselves in regard to what they think or feel. For this reason, many people become uncomfortable when you admit that you are afraid. "You just need to push past your fears," is the advice we all have heard. First of all, if we could, we would have already done so. Second, when we say push past our fears, are we not simply telling people to ignore their fears?

The fact of the matter is that we cannot ignore our fears. Sure, we can waste a lot of our energy trying to deny that they exist, yet they will always resurface. The truth is they will resurface in greater intensity until we are willing to listen to the underlying message. For this reason, it will be supportive to have people who are able to sit with fear.

When we have a fear, we are best serving ourselves if we come to understand what the fear is about. At first, this may feel overwhelming, because we are not used to listening to our fears. Yet anyone who can sit with us, validate that what we are feeling is normal, and support us to look at what the fear is really about will be helping us significantly.

Admitting to Ourselves When We Are Fearful

When we begin admitting out loud that we are afraid, it is important to notice our own reaction. Often times we will feel a surge of energy. In fact, a part of us will recognize that in owning our fear, we are actually claiming our power. This occurs because we are no longer fighting ourselves. Instead of our energy going toward trying to push down or deny that we are afraid, we allow ourselves that feeling.

Although a part of us may feel empowered by owning our fear, another part of us will still feel afraid. What do we do with that fear? We listen. Once we are able to allow ourselves to feel afraid, we will find that there are many gifts being presented to us. Besides recognizing our power, we will also have the opportunity to detach ourselves emotionally from what we are hearing about ourselves. Our ability to open ourselves to those messages will demonstrate where we are in the process of discovering our truth.

Let us use the example of being afraid of failing, since this is a common fear, whether the fear is work related or about a relationship. If we are afraid of failing, our voice of fear will likely tell us how inadequate we are in some way. This fear is actually there to alert us that we are looking outside ourselves to feel valued, worthy, or accepted. In other words, our fear is kicking in because we are giving our power away.

One of my clients was doing just that when he felt stalled with his career. Because he did not have a college degree, he felt that his opportunities to move any further were limited. He also felt boxed in at his current job, as he was afraid others would not consider him for a higher paid position due to his inability to finish college. His fears, as are most of our fears, were self-imposed. No one shared with him that he could not get promoted because he did not finish college. He was recalling how he felt when he first struggled getting a job along with those messages that he heard growing up such as being a "slacker."

Our work together was about reclaiming his truth. In order to do this, we had to separate truth from fiction. The reason his fears had such a hold on him, as they do all of us, is because a part of him was emotionally tied to the fictional story. Internally he questioned his worthiness and value, which were tied to how others perceived him. When he was trying to prove himself to those in his past who did not see his potential, he was caught in the fear. The fear kept him stalled, because the truth was that no matter what he did, he would never feel like he would be good enough to those who looked down on him. When he was to check back in with his internal sense of self and reflect on all that he created despite not finishing his degree, he felt pride again in his abilities, talents, and sense of self. Because he regained his sense of confidence, he was offered a promotion that rekindled his love for his career.

The purpose of our fears is to call us to check in with ourselves. If we listen to what the fear is telling us and believe in being inadequate, that is where we need to begin. Feeling like we lack worth in some way is our Spirit's way to get us in enough pain that we are willing to face our truth. Our truth is that we are worthy just in our being. If we do not recognize this, we will have to continue to work with our emotions to find our truth. (This will be discussed more thoroughly in the following chapter.) Our fear is present to guide us back to our truth and to remind us when we are looking to the external to get validated. Our fear is also there to guide us as to how to give to ourselves what we are looking for outside of ourselves.

Recently I freaked out about aging. After feeling very content with myself for years, my reaction was quite shocking –it seemed like the old me had resurfaced. The truth was there was a part me that was holding on to an old image of myself that I had not yet let go of. There was this fragment of me who wanted to feel validated, accepted, and loved based on my appearance. After crying about this for hours, I realized what this was about for me. It was about me accepting myself as the new woman I have become.

Even though most of me honored who I am, there was a part of me wanting to keep a version of my physically younger self. Although my fear told me I was upset because I felt others saw me as old and unattractive, I could hear my truth once I let out my anguish. All the anguish and tears was really from my Spirit wanting me to recognize my beauty and worth for who I am now and not for who I used to be. Now I have come to find the gift in my wrinkles, as they demonstrate a woman who has insights based on her experiences, is settled in her skin, and likes what she sees internally as well as externally. This is an example of the gifts that are disguised as our fears.

Through befriending my fears, I have found the guidance I need to move me forward with my life. Whether it is with myself, relationships, or professional pursuits, through listening to the underlying message of my fears, I am guided. My fears worked over time in order for me to be willing to have the courage to write this book. I heard the same messages I have heard many times before I could recognize that voice for what it is.

The Universe makes it very easy for us to differentiate between our fear and our truth. Our fear is always blunt and mean spirited, which is quite a recognizable difference from our truth. Our truth is there to support us and not belittle us.

Our fear will say things such as, "You suck, you are incredibly incompetent, you are worthless." Our ego has us buy into a notion that our Spirit is so nice that without it, we would not get the constructive criticism that we need to move forward. However, if our Spirit needs to guide us to make change, it will. We would hear our Spirit in a much more gentle way than if our ego were pushing us to change.

Recently my inner voice relayed this message to me: "Notice how nervous you were when you speak. It will be of benefit to you to continue practicing speaking. The Universe will give you further opportunity to develop that skill. Trust and have faith, as you are on your way." Within a few months, I had enormous amounts of opportunities that gave me the confidence I desired.

The difference between the voice of our fear coming from our ego and that of our truth coming from our Spirit is easily recognizable. *We do not need that dictating and critical voice of our ego to serve us to get our desired outcome in life.* The message of our truth is always guiding us to stay true to ourselves and our path. When we trust in our inner voice, that is when we feel the magic occurring in our life, as our experiences are better than we expected.

Now when I hear fear, I say to myself, "Oh, yes, that is my voice of fear, which means I am on my way to expanding!" Because I know the truth of my fears, a part of me feels excited, as I know I am embarking on a new adventure. I am excited, because I recognize that my Spirit is guiding me to own more of my truth and power in order for me to manifest all my desires.

Our fears are trustworthy companions on our journey, telling us when we are looking outside of ourselves to have our needs met. Our fears are serving us by being an alarm, warning us that we are trying to gain approval, validation, or love in a manner that will not fulfill us. When we are going outside of ourselves for our needs, this is based on us allowing our egos to guide us. However, if we listen to the guidance underneath the fears, we are always being directed to go back to our inner truth, which is guided by our Spirit. Our Spirit desires us to live our best life and will support us through our fears to have what we need internally in order for us to create our ideal life.

Putting this Chapter into Practice:

1) What do you fear about yourself? What is it that you say you would never want to be like? Know that you are manifesting those behaviors in your life because

you are not accepting of them. Look for ways that you can accept that quality about yourself. Admitting how you exhibit those behaviors will give you more compassion toward yourself and others, which shifts the fear from having such a tight hold over you.

2) Look at yourself in the mirror. Try not to look at your face but concentrate on the depth of your eyes. What thoughts come to mind? Notice if your first reaction is to judge yourself or if certain feelings come forth. Whatever thoughts or feelings you have, take note as to whether they are in congruence with your Spirit. Begin to have a nurturing conversation with yourself through your eyes as you acknowledge how amazing you are just for living in this existence!

3) When you encounter a fear, allow yourself to feel it. In that way, you will release your emotional attachment to the fearful thought. Once you have allowed yourself to feel, see if you can begin to hear your inner voice. Examine how you are looking outward for approval. Journal and ask your inner voice for support as to how you can begin giving yourself the approval you desire. Wait and listen. Within the next day or two, you will be given guidance through experiences, thoughts, and feelings to guide you to understanding.

Chapter 5
Emotions and Our Pain

Through shining the light on some of our fears, as we did in the last two chapters, we may have been able to change some of our perceptions to create greater harmony with who we truly are. Many of our deep-rooted fears, however, will not change that easily. Our deep-rooted fears are those imbedded in our emotions. In other words, emotionally we buy into our fears as being the truth, even though logically we can understand that they are false. Again for this reason, utilizing "positive thinking" alone will not work. We need to be willing to unearth and understand the underlying emotions that accompany those fears.

Our emotions are our key to understanding our fears. Our emotions depict to us the specific feeling we get when we are confronted with an experience that elicits fear within us. By attending to our emotions, we can understand and move away from living our life based on fear. As we move away from the self-imposed limitations that our fears create in our lives, we will recognize how much freer we feel. In order to free ourselves from being held captive to our fears, we need to be willing to trust in the wisdom of our emotions to support us to live optimally.

Learning to Attend to Our Emotional Pain

Our body can be self-healing if we allow it to be. By giving our wounds the proper care, we heal. Depending on the degree of our injury, we seek professional assistance. We can easily witness our body's natural ability to heal with our physical ailments. Our body mends, reconfigures, and adapts.

A cut that is properly nurtured is gone in a few days. By attending to our physical wounds, we can address what is not functioning properly in order to gain back our physical well-being.

We know our body is not functioning properly when we feel physical pain. Our pain is the mechanism there to support us to recognize that our body is not functioning well. In other words, our pain is a built-in alarm system telling us that there is something wrong. We can ignore the pain, and, as a result, our physical condition will likely worsen, or we can address our pain in order to improve our body's functioning.

Just as we feel physical pain when we are not well physically, we also have emotional pain to alert us when our emotional well-being is not functioning optimally. Although this is a simple concept, most of us have been conditioned to ignore or push aside our emotions rather than attend to them. For many people, it takes having a traumatic experience in order for them to address their emotions. However, for most of us, our emotional wounds start off small. These small wounds continue to grow due to our continued neglect of our feelings.

Typically we become wounded at some point during our youth because we and those around us have no idea how to handle our feelings. Our parents struggle with being able to address our feelings because it is more challenging to recognize when we may have been impacted emotionally by an experience than physically. With young children, it can be tricky to figure out a physical ailment even when there are some visible signs. The emotional signs may be even more subtle, which makes figuring out another's feelings very perplexing at times. Parents also may not address a child's feelings because many parents do not know how to handle their own emotions, let alone their children's. If parents do not have compassion for their own feelings, it makes being able to recognize or respect other people's pain even more difficult.

When We Do Not Address Our Pain, We Adapt

Because for many of us our emotional wounds were not addressed when we were young, we learned to adapt emotionally. Just as our body would learn how to adapt and function utilizing only one leg, our emotions are adaptive as well. When our bodies adapt physically, it is because we have no other choice. When the functioning of a part of our body is lost, often times it cannot be recovered. However, with our emotions, most of us have the ability to regain functioning so we can live our life feeling our best. Chances are that if you have picked up this book, you are ready to regain optimal emotional well-being, if you choose.

In order to live optimally, we need to address our emotional pain, just as we would our physical pain. Unfortunately, many of us are unconscious of our emotional pain because we have gotten too good at ignoring the signals that are telling us we are not doing well. Just as we would lose consciousness if we stayed in a great degree of pain for an extended period, our emotional system must do the same in order for us to survive. By learning to address our feelings, we begin to become conscious again about how we are living our lives. Being honest with our feelings, regardless of what they are, is the first step.

Our Feelings Are Our Body's Natural Way of Regaining Balance

Our body naturally is able to bring us to our optimal emotional health when we honor our feelings. We can understand the depth of how issues are affecting us by paying attention to the degree of pain within our emotions. Some experiences are not that emotionally painful, and when we express how the experience made us feel, we can easily move toward feeling emotionally balanced again. Other experiences may have caused us more pain; with those, we will have a greater depth to our emotions. The greater the degree of our pain, the more is being revealed to us how much an experience has impacted our emotional well-being. Regardless of how "small" we may feel the issue was, our Spirit was obviously impacted in a negative way due to the depth of feeling related to the event. The point is that no issue is too small to be of significance for our Spirit. Our Spirit wants us to always be aligned with our truth. Being aware of even the smallest circumstance that causes us pain can support us to create the balanced life we desire to live.

Most of us learn exactly the opposite regarding our feelings. We are told to "get over it" or "move on," especially when an issue seems small to another person. When another says this to us, it is because he or she cannot handle our emotions. It does not mean that there is something wrong with how we are feeling. Nevertheless, the onus gets placed on us to get rid of how we are feeling. Often times, getting rid of our feelings means pushing them down inside of us. On the outside, we appear as if we are over the situation, yet inside we are still impacted.

Even with how aware I am of the importance of emotions, I can still at times give the message to my children to move on from their feelings. When this occurs, it is because, in that moment, I, too, cannot handle their feelings. I am in a hurry, too tired, or trying to attend to something else, and I get caught up in the moment rather than addressing what is going on for them. This is not my intention, yet it still happens. Nevertheless, I work toward giving them the room to share their true feelings, because their expression allows for insight, understanding, and compassion for their own and others' feelings.

We must remind ourselves that when we release our emotions, we are permitting ourselves to recognize the real significance an issue had for us. Just letting out our emotions alone can be relieving, which is why many of us feel better after a good cry. We feel better because we are no longer carrying the weight of trying to bury these feelings deep within us. Instead, our feelings have been freed and acknowledged, which also frees the energy we were using to keep the emotions pushed down within ourselves.

Often times through our releasing process, we also gain further clarity as to why the experience impacted us the way it did. Any message or clarity that we gain from the experience is significant for us to utilize in order for us to move forward in our lives. After acknowledging our feelings, we have a choice to continue to run our life in the same manner or to make some necessary changes. Just as when we go through a physical ailment, we may need to change aspects of our living in order to maintain a healthy body, we will also need to create changes within our lives to support our emotional well being.

Creating changes, whether for our physical or emotional health, is up to us–no one else can do it for us. We must be willing to see the experiences in our lives that have caused us pain. The only way to resolve this pain is to create change. If we are willing to create change toward being more aligned with our Spirit, our pain will dissolve. If we choose to keep going about life in the same manner and do not create any changes, we will most likely experience more pain. Any further pain we experience will have the same theme to our past pain in order for us to be able to recognize that how we are going about our lives needs to be changed. Psychologists call recreating painful experiences a vicious cycle. We create these vicious cycles in order that we may finally be in enough pain to be willing to make the changes that are necessary for our emotional well-being.

From a spiritual perspective, our pain is really telling us that we are not living in alignment with our truth. When we do not listen to our truth, we feel pain. We will continue to create and feel pain until we are willing to listen to and live from our truth. We create the same type of experiences in order for us to recognize that not living in our truth does not feel good. We then have the opportunity to look at those experiences and reflect on how we could have handled ourselves differently in order to create different results.

How many times have we left a situation saying, "I wish I would have said X or done Y?" Or maybe we did not know how to handle the situation, yet we knew it did not feel good to us. Those scenarios occurred in order to help us to recognize the need to make changes to live more in alignment with our truth. We will then be given similar opportunities in the future to practice saying exactly how we feel or demonstrate our feelings through our actions. If we allow ourselves to share our truth, we will recognize how much better we feel. If we still do not express ourselves authentically, we will continue to create those vicious cycles in our lives. Thus, the gift of emotional pain is to continually realign ourselves with our truth, in order that we live a life based on our inner guidance and nothing else.

What About Using Psychotropic Medications to Help Relieve Our Pain?

Psychotropic medications can be used to help people cope with clinically diagnosed mental health symptoms such as mood, anxiety, psychotic, or dissociative disorders. The most widely used psychotropic drugs are used to help cope with symptoms of anxiety and depression. Utilizing these drugs helps patients to not feel the emotions that are causing them distress. Unfortunately, the medications may also inhibit a person's pleasurable experiences as well, whether those are mood related, such as a sense of joy or passion toward living, or physically related, such as one's sex drive.

Should these medications be used? It depends. If you are unable to function at all, meaning you literally cannot get out of bed each day, it may be something that you consider. In a case such as this, you need to be able to treat the symptom in order that you are able to manage the circumstances that are gravely impacting you. Once you have regained functioning,

I would suggest working toward alleviating the cause of the symptom. For some people, the idea of alleviating the root of the emotional symptoms is controversial because they believe that their mental symptoms are due to a genetic predisposition, i.e. "it runs in the family." My personal opinion is that we can have temperament traits that we could inherit that increase our susceptibility to being challenged with mental health conditions. In addition, we also "inherit" behavioral patterns through our families that may not be supporting us to address our emotions in a way that is for our highest good.

Regardless of whether you believe in nature versus nurture as the cause, the majority of people who function well in their day-to-day living are best served to attend to their emotional pain rather than cover up the symptoms. If covering up the pain through medications only leads to further problems, such as a loss in sex drive or loss of passion toward living, know that the Universe is setting these conditions up in order that we become willing to address the core of the issue. Because it is our fear of the symptoms that keeps us from wanting to experience our feelings, having support through a psychotherapist you trust will be imperative. I personally have a hard time with doctors who see patients for 10 or 15 minutes and feel comfortable with prescribing medications, including some that are highly addictive.

Where most people become stuck is in their view of wanting to "get rid" of the feelings that they consider a problem. Being able to sit with our feelings, regardless of what they are, is the first step to overcoming the fear that we are unable to cope with the emotions we are experiencing. It can be one of the most frightening experiences we have when we allow our emotions to continue to pour through us. Being willing to address your deep rooted feelings may mean that you are being called to go to the depths of your pain over and over again. Through doing so, however, we always find our way through it and back to our truth, which allows us to find the internal balance we seek.

Having lived for years with anxiety and suicidal thoughts, I can with certainty share that working with our emotions is worth it. There are many ups and downs to the process. Yet each down experience, especially those in which you are brought to the depths of your pain, will shed the light on your innermost truth.

As I discuss how pain may actually be used to support us, I am brought to thinking about another example in which I needed to be present with my physical pain. Throughout my pregnancy with my twins, I had planned on doing a home birth again. When they came seven weeks early, we rushed to the hospital. I was in such immense pain, I did not think I could withstand it. It was coming so quickly and intensely, more-so than with my previous birth. My fear was that I would not be able to withstand this amount of pain for as long as I had to with my firstborn, which was about nineteen hours. My midwife told me to hold on until she got there and shared with me that when the pain is that intense, it just means the babies were coming fast. As soon as she got there, she used natural remedies to help soothe my discomfort. Just having her there with me eased many of my fears.

She was correct that my babies were coming fast, and the doctors and nurses were completely unprepared when my first son was birthed. My other son decided he was not so sure about coming out, and the doctor struggled for sixteen minutes after the birth of my first son due to my second son being breech. Afterward the doctor shared with me how close we were to having a C-section. He told me that if I had been numb and not able to feel the pain, I would not have been able to know the exact moment when the contraction finished - that was when I needed to push.

I recognized with both our emotions and our physical bodies how pain is created to guide us. If the pain becomes more than we can bear, our bodies have a way to shut us down in order that we no longer feel it. I am not into people suffering or going through unnecessary pain. It is a blessing that we have the medical miracles that we do in order to support people to heal with less discomfort. However, there is a fine line between diminishing pain and learning how to withstand degrees of pain that are ultimately there to serve us.

My own personal experiences of struggling with my emotions in addition to becoming scared during giving birth taught me two huge lessons. The first is having experienced support to guide you is one of the best gifts to give to yourself. Surround yourself only with those who desire what you desire so that you are embraced by their love. Second, I learned that we are more powerful than we know. I see this now in others as I see how they are willing to become very uncomfortable in order to create the life they are intended to live.

All of Our Emotions Are to Support Us to Live Optimally
Many times I have dealt with people who are afraid to show their feelings because they label their emotions. Emotions that bring them joy, happiness, playfulness, or silliness are labeled as "good." Our "bad" emotions, there-fore, are our anger, sadness, loneliness, or sense of emptiness. Because we label those emotions as bad, we have learned to feel shameful about feeling any of those ways. Thus, we try to pretend that those "bad" feelings don't exist in us at all. After all, we have all witnessed damaging events when those "bad" emotions have been expressed. On the surface, it appears that life would be better without having to deal with those "bad" emotions whatsoever. However, our Spirit knows better.

Emotional Shadows
Emotions are there to guide us to free our energy. When someone says something to us and it pushes our buttons, we are emotionally impacted. Internally, as well as sometimes

externally, we are "revved-up" and feel a need to defend ourselves. We feel this need to defend ourselves because a part of us emotionally buys into what the other person is saying about us.

For instance, if we are called selfish by someone and feel greatly offended, it is because a part of our emotional selves has bought into that belief. Furthermore, we judge ourselves negatively because a part of us believes that we *are* selfish. Hence, our energy is put toward trying to prove to ourselves and others that we are not selfish.

Because of our judgment toward ourselves that we are selfish, we specifically try to put others first and be considerate. Our underlying motive to be considerate of others, however, does not come from our truth. Rather, our motive to be considerate is about demonstrating we are not selfish. Because our motive comes from our ego and our fear of being selfish, our actions result in us actually being selfish, as we are only involved with our own image.

How do we become selfish when we are trying to be considerate? Our "consideration" is really about us being self-involved, as we are trying to fill our own need to be considered a "good" person. Therefore, even in our attempts to be considerate, people will energetically feel that the focus is not about them but us. Even though we may *think* we are being considerate, others will *feel* that the experience is all about ourselves. Thus, when we judge ourselves and cannot accept aspects of ourselves, we unconsciously bring out those qualities within ourselves that we perceive as negative. Because we are unable to recognize that we create these experiences in our lives, this is known as our "shadow" side.

We will continue to create experiences in which our "shadow" shines through until we are willing to accept those aspects of ourselves that we are trying to deny. We can only learn to accept all parts of ourselves by recognizing our truth. First, whether we like it or not, these aspects of ourselves are our truth. In fact, these qualities are heightened within us when we try to deny that they exist. Second, we must learn to recognize the judgments we place on ourselves due to having certain qualities within ourselves.

Let us go back to the selfish example. What about being selfish do we judge? The key to being able to accept this quality is to recognize the benefits. In other words, we need to be willing to ask ourselves how being selfish serves us. Learning to see the truth of whatever aspect of ourselves we try to deny will allow us to energetically set ourselves free of the judgments we carry. As for being selfish, we may fear being self-involved and then judge ourselves harshly. The truth is at times we need to have a self-focus. This is especially true if we are willing to do this inner work for creating our ideal life.

When we feel drawn to focus on ourselves, we are being guided to create inner shifts. Creating inner shifts is an act of courage, not selfishness. Our selfishness is then really self-love and self-care, qualities that are greatly missing in most people today. By taking care of our own needs, we are not looking to others to fill them. When our needs are met, we have more energy to put out into the world, as our energy is freed from trying to prove we are something we are not. This energy is unstoppable, as it comes from our hearts rather than our ego.

Being able to see how we judge ourselves and others allows us to recognize how our energy has been going to our ego rather than our truth. Because it is our ego's job to hide that which we cannot handle, it is our responsibility to decide when we are willing to acknowledge all aspects of ourselves. Until we do, we are guaranteed that the aspects we do not accept will be forefront in our lives. Thus, the choice is ours: whether we want those qualities that we judge to run us or for us to be able to honor the part of us that is there to ultimately serve our highest good. Once we remember that how we are feeling is present to allow us to create shifts that guide us to create our best life, we will have less fear in accepting all aspects of ourselves.

When we can accept ourselves, we will not take a comment so personally, even if it was meant to cause us harm. From being in our own place of pain in the past, we will recognize that if a hurtful comment is made, it is due to the other person's pain. Being able to recognize this in others will support us to help resolve conflicts.

From a spiritual perspective, there is no need to label events, people, or aspects of ourselves or others. As we accept emotions, we are able to realize that our feelings are just tools to help us know the magnificence of who we are when we live our life authentically in our truth. God created every aspect of us and life in order to help us develop to our highest potential. It makes sense then that our Creator did not create within us any "bad" emotions. Each emotion, therefore, is there to help us not only recognize when we are aligned with our Spirit but also how to get back to living that way.

Recently my "shadow button" was pushed during a yoga session. The instructor wanted me to do a movement that felt very challenging to me. I was doing my best yet still felt stuck with being able to correct my posture. She was unable to give me directives to support me, so instead she kept reiterating what I was doing wrong. As I heard myself say, "I cannot do this," tears welled up in my eyes. I had bought into an old wound that even when I try my best, it is not enough.

I have not seen this wound in years, so I was in shock that I was tearing up during my class. I was angry at the instructor for not being able to guide me, but most of all my tears were about the sadness of acknowledging an old pain that still existed within me. I saw myself acting out of sorts, and I would freeze up as my instructor came by me and I was unable to speak my truth. I just went along with feeling inadequate.

This shadow was not about what my instructor said, it was about having a painful experience recreated. It was that feeling that I was not measuring up to others' expectations–and I crumbled. In other words, I crumbled not because of what she did but because of my reaction to her. I went back to a state of wanting to please and do a good enough job so that I had given away my power. As I did, that is when my tears flowed. My truth is that I still give my power away at times to please others, to feel liked and accepted. Even though I do this much less often, my Spirit needed me to know that this still happens. The gift is being able to recognize how, why, and under what circumstances I tend to give my power away in order to make the appropriate adjustments in my future. The Universe does this in order that I may live my life fully and at ease. Through my shadow button being pushed, I am able to utilize my emotional reaction to guide me to live more deeply from my truth.

We need to know each of our emotions in order to experience what living a powerful, loving, and abundant life feels like. If we were simply given all that we desired, we would not feel the true joy in having it. In being able to experience the opposite of what we desire, we are able to fully receive the gifts that we are all entitled to have in life. In order for us to accept abundance, we must be willing to allow in each emotion and understand its purpose toward creating the life we truly desire to live.

Moving from Anxiety to Feeling at Peace

Anxiety is caused when we are not willing to listen to the guidance we receive. We are too caught up in our head trying to figure out the matter logically. What we do not realize when this is occurring is that not all matters were meant to be resolved by our logic. We forget that our mind is just a part of our body designed to support us to make decisions. Unfortunately, we have become overly reliant on our mind, intellect, and logic, to a fault. We falter because the issue can be easily resolved if we were to listen to what our inner voice has to say about the matter. If we do not listen, however, we feel anxious because we are not able to wrap our heads around the full perspective that is necessary to make the decision that is in our best interest. A sure sign that we are over-utilizing our logic is our anxiety, as it is sharing with us that we are ignoring the inner voice that is trying to guide us.

When we initially try to listen to our inner voice, we often feel challenged because we are not certain where that thought is coming from if it does not make sense to us. When this occurs, we can ask our inner voice to give us greater clarity. Our inner voice gives us messages that are spoken gently to us, because this is the voice that is tapped into our spiritual connection. Our ego, on the other hand, tends to sound like a tyrant trying to control us. If we keep getting gentle, repetitive thoughts or ideas, then those are the messages our inner voice is trying to get across to us. We also need to pay attention to the signs and clues brought to us through other people or messages we see and hear while we are thinking about our dilemma. Of course, our mind can easily dismiss these instances, yet these are the ways in which we get support on a spiritual level.

We are all given support, but it is up to us as to ask for help and be open to what we receive. We need to also keep in mind that just because we are receiving guidance from our soul, or inner voice, this does not mean that we will like what it is telling us. When we ask, we need to be willing to listen and then take action. This may prove to be challenging for us if we do not like the guidance we are receiving. Yet when we take action toward following our inner voice, we will find peace.

It is important for us to recognize that the purpose of anxiety is so that we are not in a state of peace at all times. The anxiety is present to help us. Of course, we do not want to be living a high-strung life. Most of us desire to feel at peace most of the time. However, when those times come that bring us a sense of anxiety and/or restlessness, honor them to create movement in our lives. When we take action, there is no more need for the anxiety. The purpose of anxiety, which is to motivate us to move toward the direction our souls want to take us, will have been completed through taking the necessary steps to reach a goal. After the steps are completed, we may feel freedom, peace, or a sense of releasing.

When we first bring about change, life may not feel very peaceful. Yet we can go about change in a more peaceful manner by allowing in our guidance, trusting it, and following through with what we received. In doing so, we can at least be more at peace that the direction we are heading in is the one that is right for us, regardless of whether it makes sense to ourselves or others. Having this trust and belief that we are cared for and guided will allow us to attain all that we desire in life. We are abundantly blessed with guidance when we create a committed relationship to connecting with our Source rather than focusing on our limited thinking.

Even writing this section was divine guidance for me today. In order to hear this guidance, I had to make myself open to receiving the wisdom of my inner voice in order to receive the message. The message I got through a thought in my head was "write about peace today." This message did not come with trumpets or even in a different voice. It was my own voice. How then did I recognize this thought as the divine guidance of my inner voice? I knew I was receiving divine guidance because peace was the last thing on my mind.

As I began to work this morning on this book, I was feeling anxious about all that I want to accomplish and how to go about doing it. I was becoming worried about how to balance my work schedule over the holidays, feel connected with my family, and still take care of all that needed to get done. I certainly was not in a state of peace, and therefore thought I would have nothing to say about being peaceful today. Nevertheless, I was guided to write about peace. Now I see I was guided in this manner in order to share my struggle and give understanding to anxiety as well as how to overcome its power over us.

Anxiety exists in order to bring us back to peace. Allow ourselves to listen to what we are being told and we will find our way back to the peace that we desire. We are all loved, and it is only up to us to allow ourselves to receive and follow the loving guidance that will lead us to joyful living.

The Gift of Vulnerability

When we feel vulnerable, we often feel powerless, afraid, and maybe even ashamed. We feel vulnerable because we are trying to mask our truth. What is challenging for us to recognize is that when we feel vulnerable, we are actually receiving a choice to either face our fears by sharing our truth or to continue to hide our truth. Unfortunately, many of us continue to hide our truth.

I remember not too long ago when I was just starting out my coaching work: I was asked by an acquaintance how many clients I had. Although it was a simple and nonthreatening question, I felt threatened. That question represented to me my lack of talent, because I was not as successful as I would have liked to be. (Notice my reaction was based on my own judgment of myself, not hers.) I was so afraid that if she knew the truth, which was that I only had one client, she would certainly have judged me as harshly as I judged myself.

Before I recognized what was coming out of my mouth, I lied. I flat out lied! I could not believe it when it happened. Instead of telling her the truth that I had one client, I told her I had two. Lying about having two clients instead of one was so absurd if I had thought about it rationally. It is not as if having two clients would make me a more legitimate coach. Furthermore, I could not believe I lied. Lying, whether you call it a white lie or a big whopper, goes against all my principles, karma, and what I teach my clients. Yet there I was trying to rationalize how I "sort of" had two clients just to make myself feel better.

The truth was that *I* was ashamed and judged myself for having only one client. No one else judged me for this. In fact, most people could not believe that I had time for anything besides taking care of my three young children. Nevertheless, I felt ashamed and vulnerable from a simple question because I was not honoring my own self-worth. I was tying my worth based upon how many clients I had, rather than knowing I am an amazing being just for who I am. Instead of knowing my magnificence, I felt I lost the connection to my truth because I was judging myself as not being good enough. (As I stated earlier, these old recordings are very deeply embedded in our psyche, whether we are aware of it or not). As I found out, turning to the external to try to receive a sense of inner value always ends up cutting us off from our Source.

Being able to step back from my own situation and give it some perspective, as I would have with my clients, I could be more compassionate. Through my compassion, I could see value in myself and others just through living life the best I know how. I could also see value through the many ways in which I was living in alignment with my Spirit. I reminded myself to trust in the Universe's plan as well. Not having as many clients as I desired might really be a gift so I could focus my energy in different places.

I feel blessed to have had the experience of lying through my teeth, even at a stage where I felt I was very good at living in my truth. It demonstrated to me that although we strive throughout our journey to always be in alignment with our Source, we are also all human. We all have vulnerabilities. Even though it is part of my job to help people address their vulnerabilities, I continue to have moments of feeling vulnerable myself. What I find is that these experiences allow me to be a better at my work, as I am reminded how quickly our fears can blindside us and take over our perspective, feelings, and actions. Being a person who desires to stay aligned with my Spirit, it is my responsibility to recognize what brings me to feeling vulnerable. Once I can address the areas that make me feel vulnerable, I must acknowledge how I am buying into beliefs that are not my truth.

Allowing ourselves to be vulnerable with our feelings will help us recognize that we are looking for the external to validate us, which causes the ego to take over. Because I turn my back on myself, my truth, the ego steps in and tries to cover my shame. The mask my ego creates no longer feels good or safe, which tells me I need to check-in with myself. As I reconnect to my inner knowingness, I realize the pain I cause myself when I want the external to validate me rather than giving myself that inner sense of value, worth, and love.

If we were to share our feelings of not being enough or worthy or deserving or however we feel we are lacking, we will begin to see the absurdity. It becomes absurd because it is such an old, old tape of ours that plays over and over again throughout our lives. If we choose to share this with someone we trust, we will see that on some level, it is almost laughable and silly how we continue to discount our worth. The story is so old and boring it would put us to sleep if we were watching a movie.

As we laugh about the silliness of our egos and the traps they get us into, we let our defenses down. We no longer have to pretend we have it all together or we are perfect. When we can laugh or cry with another when we feel vulnerable, we are really opening ourselves up to a gift. This gift is demonstrating our humanness to another, which allows people to connect with us just as we are. People will be able to connect with us because they will appreciate our honesty and vulnerability. Being vulnerable dissolves the masks we created in order to protect our egos. As our masks unveil our truth, we are able to connect to one another as spiritual beings doing our best in this human experience.

Knowing that others can connect with us regardless of what we may have said or done is a wonderful gift. It is also a gift to be able to step back and review the impact that our tapes have on our life. Again, we are being shown the option to continue to believe in those tapes or to know our truth. Allowing others to see us when we are vulnerable tears apart our fear that if we show our true selves, we will be an outcast. Our feelings of vulnerability also open our hearts to recognize with compassion when others fall victim to their egos. When we learn to share our truth, regardless of our ego's fear of us becoming vulnerable and showing who we truly are, we become free. Having that freedom is powerful!

Allowing Ourselves to Be Stuck Will Support Us to Move Authentically

Feeling stuck is actually a great place to be, although when you are stuck, it does not feel good at all. Why then would being stuck be good? We have to be stuck enough to be willing to take the necessary actions toward whatever it is our soul desires from us. Again, this is like pain. Just as pain does not feel good, the discomfort eventually supports us to make different choices. Feeling stuck is another form of pain. Being stuck can feel like a more subtle pain at first, but the more stuck we become, the greater the pain will be.

Being stuck represents that we are unwilling at the time to create the necessary changes that will bring us peace and happiness. Being stuck is good, because when we recognize this feeling, we can allow ourselves to reflect on our lives. We begin to question what is and is not working in our lives. Through this process, we can acknowledge what areas we need and desire to change. Being stuck long enough will allow us to explore different avenues for making this change occur.

Many times being stuck creates enough pain to force us to take the path that we are most resisting. In all likelihood, we will first try the most convenient way of addressing being stuck, which is by placing blame on others and trying to make them change. Regardless of whether they change or not, we will remain stuck, because others truly do not have control over our happiness.

Blame is just another form of being the victim. Being the victim takes away our ability to take responsibility for our lives. It is not until we are willing to take responsibility for our lives that we can become unstuck. Sometimes the word "responsibility" and what it implies can feel overwhelming to us. If we break down the word "responsibility" to mean *respond to my ability*, taking responsibility for our lives feels less scary. We avoid taking responsibility for our lives because we do not feel that we know the "right" action to take. This is how we become stuck. However, responding to our ability does not mean that we have to have the "right" answer. It simply means we must respond to and address what is not working for us as we best know how to in that moment. When we are willing to be responsible for our lives, we are taking back our power to create change in our life. The gift of being stuck is therefore to allow us to recognize that we actually do have the power to make our life as we desire it to be.

The power we have is to choose. We can continue to do what we have been doing, which will keep us feeling stuck. On the other hand, we can choose to do something completely different, something that stretches us outside of our comfort zone in order to feel that we are creating movement in our lives again. When we are no longer stagnant, we create possibilities and opportunities. When we are stagnant, there is no room to create.

We are creative beings who long to keep manifesting. This is why we get restless after a while. We go through challenges, create a long-time desire, and, not too shortly thereafter, are ready for more. Our Spirit wants us to recognize all that we are capable of manifesting. This is why we love being creators, because it is a part of who we are.

We have all seen people who by society's standards have a really nice life. One of my clients was just this type of person. He did not come from a family who had a lot or even believed that it was possible for him to be able to have much in life. When he was young, he did okay in school, but his family looked at him in many ways as a mess. However, when he was willing to take responsibility for his life, he did just that and worked his way to becoming very successful in sales. For two decades of his life, he committed himself to achieving success at his job, and he did well for himself. He did better than he or his family ever thought was possible. By all accounts, he had a very nice life.

This man came to me, however, because he felt he lacked passion for living. He had worked so hard to manifest his career, and now he was feeling burned out and stuck. This is because he was no longer creating! His soul was longing for him to create again. He had manifested an amazing career for himself, and now all he had to do was basically maintain this lifestyle. Maintaining and doing the same thing day after day is boring to our souls. We cannot feel alive doing the same thing day in and day out. It is in creating that we feel joy, and we feel movement because we become alive again when we create.

I, too, have a recent example of feeling stuck. I was feeling stuck when it came to my career. I knew I wanted to jumpstart my career again, yet I felt stuck as to how to do it. I tried some avenues that did not generate the response that I desired. I felt exasperated trying to figure out what I had to do in order to create the career I desired. After a time of playing the victim, I decided I had enough of hearing my same complaints about myself and life over and over again. After yet another tearful experience of ranting and raving about how much I do not nor ever will measure up, I decided not to buy into the excuses anymore and take action.

Of course, when I was stuck, I did not feel like I was making excuses at all. "This is just how God wants my life to be," I told myself. Telling myself this gave me a week or two of peace until that unsettling feeling came back. Inside, I continued to feel restless and would question myself and my abilities. I questioned and critiqued myself over and over and over again, causing myself a lot of pain. Beating myself up allowed me to keep going about life in the same way because I was making myself the victim. When we continue to tell ourselves how we are not good enough and all the reasons why, we are really just allowing ourselves to feel like the victim of our life. Nothing could be further from the truth.

I could only discover my truth, however, by being able to see how beating myself up was in no way serving me. I had to stop and ask how my perspective and actions were supporting me toward my desires. Obviously they were not. They were excuses to keep me from moving forward, and I got tired of it. I saw how my feelings and fears were my protection from taking full responsibility for creating the life I desired.

After I was able to take in how I was hurting myself, I then recognized that I had a choice. I could keep doing what I was doing and continue to get the same results. The other choice I had was to take more responsibility for my life by taking drastic action. As we can see, being stuck and becoming tired of it allowed me to take the necessary risks that I would have never willingly done on my own.

I needed to get stuck and for as long as I did in order to get drastic and be risky. For me this meant being willing to listen to my inner voice and wake up in the middle of the night to write. My rational mind tried to convince me that my losing sleep to write was a waste of my time. Yet, I became less scared of the risk because I could not imagine what I would actually be losing. Would I feel greater sadness if I failed or felt even like a bigger failure? No. The truth was that I was feeling like a failure *because I was not trying.* I was not moving. I was stagnant and no longer creating as I played the victim. Even though playing the victim is a creation in and of itself, it was a role that I have played too many times for it to be fun anymore. In my mind, I finally reached my pinnacle of realizing that I had no other choice but to take risks toward making my desires actually happen rather than continue to diminish their possibility of ever existing.

Being the victim and being stuck helped me to gain the courage to take action in a way that served me. Being the victim and staying stagnant gets old. Creating in a way that does not serve us is not fun either. These are truths. From being able to recognize these truths, I could see how false my being the victim was. All the ways I told myself I was not good enough to go for my dream no longer had value for me. As soon as I began to see that I had the choice to no longer buy into the shackles of being the victim, I became free from my self-imposed torture. After all, there was no time to create being the victim any more–I was too busy creating the life of my dreams.

May we remember to turn our feelings of being stuck into being willing to take the risk that our Spirit is calling for each of us to take. When we allow ourselves to listen yet again to the excuses and fears as to why we should remain going about our life in the same manner, eventually we will become tired. Be stuck, listen to our tapes over and over until they bore us. Then watch how our allowing ourselves to be sick and tired of our lives allows us to make dramatic changes. The magic then unfolds, and we feel the exhilaration of truly living life again!

Allowing Ourselves to Be Complacent in Order that We May Feel Passion!

How I am feeling right now as I write this is tired. Not physically tired but emotionally tired. I do not want to handle many of the responsibilities I have signed up for right now. I am not in the mood. I want to be alone, feel isolated, relax, retreat, unwind, and be free. I do not feel free right now because I feel too tied down to all the commitments in my life, and I do not have enough time for me–what I desire and what I want to do. All I want to do right now is nothing.

Doing nothing is blissful, because then I am without purpose. When I allow myself to let go of needing to be purposeful all the time, I actually allow in my true purpose or the purpose God intends for me. Busying myself with all the activities in my life leaves no room for me to let in, acknowledge, and become aware of my intended purpose. For this reason, I know right now I need to allow myself to just be and breathe. That is all I want to be responsible for right now–breathing.

Unfortunately, my guilt loves to get in the way of allowing me the space to just breathe. My guilt is just an extension of my ego. My ego, of course, wants me to believe that my worth is based on all I do. My truth knows that my worth is inherent because I am a part of God.

When my guilt tries to take over, I hear the word "should" quite often. I should be doing X and should not be doing Y. Usually this means that I should be doing more of the things that I do not want to do and less of the things that would bring me comfort, joy, or peace. For example, I should do household chores, pay my bills, or attend an event rather than relax, rest, and unwind like my inner voice is guiding me to do. "Should" is a great word, because it equates to meaning that what we are doing is not enough. In other words, we are not enough. Being able to recognize the truth of guilt is helpful, because then we know we do not need to buy into the lie that we "should" be doing anything other than what is authentic from us.

My clients tend to get squirmy about actually listening to their feelings about allowing themselves to do nothing. "I have responsibilities that only I can handle," they say. This is true for most of us. However, we do not need to expect ourselves to continue going about fulfilling our responsibilities to our fullest potential all the time. It is okay to allow ourselves to slack off, be lazy, and do less once in a while.

The truth is we can do less and everyone will still be okay. As a mother, I still have to take care of the basic needs of my kids. However, I do not have to overextend myself by doing laundry, making dinner, or even playing games if I do not have the energy to give. They will survive a low-energy day. In fact, we may often find that allowing ourselves low-energy days also feels good to others around us. By modeling that we are not valuing our own sense of worth based on our productivity, we demonstrate to others that it is okay and actually feels good to just be.

I have come to realize that I feel better about myself when I feel happy rather than valuing myself for how much I do. I feel happy when I give myself a break, whether that is with my work, my family, my home, or other responsibilities. By allowing myself this space to nurture myself, I restore within me the energy I desire to live my life with passion and purpose.

Many of my clients fear that if they were to allow themselves the gift of doing nothing, they would get used to it. "Good," I tell them. We all need to get used to allowing ourselves the space to do nothing. Otherwise we risk becoming so burned out that we are complacent about our lives.

We become complacent about our lives when we have nothing left to give of ourselves. Our energy is completely depleted and we are running on fumes. When our lives are on automatic pilot, when we run around taking care of all the responsibilities in our lives, we are not living. We are surviving. Living our lives by just surviving takes away the energy we need to acknowledge our feelings to create the necessary changes to bring us back to really living.

So many people I know live their lives in survival mode. It is all they know. This is because how they live is based on their fears. A common fear is the sense that I must continue to push myself or I/my family will not have enough to survive. When we live our life based on this fear of lack, we actually mirror that experience within ourselves. We are doing all we can so we do not experience lack, yet that is how we feel inside. We are lacking because we are not living. We are lacking peace, joy, and passion.

What we are also missing when we live in survival mode is our health. Emotionally we become drained and tired as the tasks that are a part of our lives become monotonous and tedious. Physically our bodies become drained as well. When we feel tired of our lives, and we do not treat ourselves well physically, we do not get adequate sleep, nurture ourselves properly, or exercise. Our Spirit will feel exhausted, too. When our body, mind, and Spirit are feeling drained, we become sick. God has designed our system to shut down in order to force us to take proper care of ourselves.

By giving in to our feelings when we desire to do nothing and take time out from our busy lives, we can enjoy a day doing an activity we love. Instead, when we have to make ourselves sick, literally, in order to get the "downtime" we need, we are stuck in bed not feeling well. The decision is ours whether our downtime is spent in bed feeling pain or, once in a while, giving ourselves space to live life free of our responsibilities.

Remember that I previously explained that responsibility means to "respond within our ability." We are not expected to respond more than our body, mind, or Spirit can handle. Allowing ourselves to be human and take the necessary breaks that we are craving will allow us to be able to respond to more of what we desire in the future.

Our fear is that if we give into our feelings of tiredness or complacency, we will become complacent. The truth is that when we fight off our feelings of complacency, we become complacent, because we are too tired to deal appropriately with our lives. What we resist persists.

When we allow ourselves to surrender to our complacency, our laziness, and our desire to escape, we are allowing ourselves to be renewed again. We are actually re-energizing ourselves. If we could not be so damn harsh with ourselves all the time and label our need to re-energize as lazy, we would have so much more life to us. We would be living! Being human is recognizing that we need to care, nurture, and fuel our Spirit. Once we are refueled, we can accomplish anything. If we are not refueled, we will not have the energy to take care of our basic needs adequately.

Anger is Our Source of Internal Power

When we feel angry, we are really feeling a loss of control. We are at "wits end," literally, because we feel as if we do not know what to do. Our anger is an expression of the frustration we feel when we are trying our best in a situation yet the circumstances are not as we would like them to be. Thus we become angry either at ourselves, others, or both.

Our anger is really about us being hurt. We are hurt that we cannot impact a situation as we would have desired. Internally we may feel useless, which triggers the old, painful wounds of not feeling that we are enough, or that we can never do things right. Depending on our circumstances, we may feel blocked from expressing our sadness because we do not have a sense of compassion for ourselves. Instead we are frustrated by ourselves and our lives.

At times when we express our anger, we may lash out at others rather than recognizing that we are hurt. In other words, we are blocking the fact that a part of us is sad. People who are prone to lashing out in anger have learned that it is weak to express that they are hurt or sad. Most likely they have had an experience in which they were caused more pain by demonstrating that they were hurt. Internally they feel powerless, yet they are attempting to convince themselves and others that they are strong in order to protect themselves from getting hurt again. They know firsthand how anger keeps others at a distance so that no one can figure out their true feelings. After all, people who actively express their anger likely learned it from an intimate source in their life. Deep down people with great anger are those who feel the most vulnerable to allow others to truly see how "weak" or hurt they actually are.

More common are people who have learned to bury most of their anger and work really hard to come across to everyone as pleasant. Deep down those people tend to be filled with rage because they have so much pain buried within them. Similar to people who express their anger openly, the overly pleasant people have also learned not to express that they are hurt. They do not feel that they need anger to protect themselves. Instead, they feel that expressing what they are feeling is futile because there is a sense that doing so would be useless. In the past, they likely expressed their feelings only to have them ignored or to feel that they lacked importance to those they shared their feelings with. Thus, they have learned that their feelings of sadness are not worthwhile to others. Of course, this causes rage within, because our inner voice knows that our feelings do matter. These feelings either explode haphazardly onto others or they remain bottled up within, causing disease and depression.

We must remember that we are touched to the core with our anger for a reason. Again, we need to feel that emotion, that surge of energy, to create changes that are necessary to our existence. Anger and frustration go hand in hand for a reason: we *should* feel frustrated by our life circumstances when we feel anger. Our anger demonstrates to ourselves that we are not mildly frustrated; rather, we are extremely frustrated. When we are extremely frustrated, it is probably because we keep getting the same results regardless of how hard we try. The problem is that we keep trying the same method over and over again, yet we are expecting that the result be different. It will not be! If we continue to do the same thing over and over, we will get the same result over and over.

Regardless of whether we express our anger freely or stuff it inside, when we feel anger and frustration, we are feeling powerless. When we express anger all the time, it is our ego that we are fueling, because our ego feels threatened. When our ego feels threatened, we utilize anger to cause pain in order to push away those who are getting too close. The more we get angry, the greater the injury is inside of us, which our ego tries to protect. When our anger comes through our attachment to ego, it does not serve us or anyone, even if we get what we want through expressing our anger. In fact, if we utilize our anger to meet our ego's need to feel better about ourselves when we feel powerless, our ability to manifest will only be further inhibited.

The reason why those who express their anger too freely do so is because they already feel a lack of connection with most others. For those who tend to push down their anger, it is because of the fear of the damage their anger could cause. As humans, we long to have connections with others. For those who fear their anger, the fear is likely based on feeling the chasm that expressing their feelings to another created in their past. Because our ego tries to protect us from our fears, we pretend to be okay in order to not create that chasm again with another. Hence, we would rather create internal pain for us to push down than to experience the pain we felt when we made ourselves vulnerable and were rejected for our anger.

When we are spiritually connected, however, our anger becomes present to demonstrate that our internal boundaries have been violated. Our anger is the internal juice, or fire, that allows us to correct those boundaries. Because our anger is connected through Spirit, we can correct our boundaries without harming another in the process. Our Spirit allows us to lovingly and firmly establish what is for our highest good. We know we are coming from love when our intention is not to cause harm to another as spite for them impacting us. From a spiritual perspective, there is no judgment about feeling angry. We need our anger, just as Jesus Christ needed it to take a stand for what was right. Others may not like the stand we take, yet we know and trust the inner guidance we are receiving to create change. Our anger is a part of our life force that allows us to create significant shifts. If we are not connected spiritually to this life force within us, we will not be able to create and manifest all that we desire.

The truth is we are extremely powerful, yet we are afraid to own up to that power within us. We are afraid to make the necessary changes, to demonstrate all our feelings, and to stand openly in our truth. Our anger is the energy of our internal power. We feel anger when we are not utilizing our power to create the life we are intended to live. Once we begin living from our truth freely, we will feel our power working for us as we create the life we desire.

Confronting the fear we have about our anger will allow us to make the shift from feeling angry and powerless to living a life filled with owning how powerful we all truly are. Once we are no longer afraid of our power and all the glory it gives us, we will no longer have the need to hide behind a sense of powerlessness by being angry. We must be willing to recognize that if we are full of rage at times, we do not have to create fear to get our needs met. For those who suppress their anger because of their fear of hurting others, recognize that in not expressing our truth, we hurt ourselves and everyone else involved by living a lie. We can address the issues that cause us frustration through a sense of love while still standing strongly in our beliefs. Our anger is then lovingly transformed into knowing the truth of who we really are. Our truth is that we are all powerful and valuable assets to everyone we touch when we own and honor our real sense of self!

Our Sadness Reveals Our Truth that Leads Us to Happiness

Sadness is an emotion that I have been very familiar with in my life. In fact, sadness used to permeate my life. Because this feeling was in my life, I used to utilize all the energy I had trying to pretend and cover up the sadness I felt inside. To the outside world, I was good at depicting that I was happy and carefree. I also was good at keeping myself very busy and creating a lot of drama in order to not have to pay attention to the sadness I felt. Nevertheless, I could not hide from my sadness because at that time in my life, sadness was my truth.

I was sad for a long time because I had lost who I really was. So badly did I want the approval of others that all my energy went toward being the type of person that they wanted me to be. My Spirit was sad because I was not being me. My sadness turned to depression when I could no longer hear my inner voice to guide me. I had replaced it with other people's voices who, I felt, knew more than me. I doubted every step I took because I was so disconnected from my true self.

What I did not realize at the time was that my sadness was a gift. My sadness was my barometer telling me that something in my life was not right. Sadness becomes present for all of us to recognize that we are not living authentically. When we are not living authentically, we cannot thoroughly feel joy, beauty, and gratitude for all of life.

Once I was able to acknowledge and honor the fact that I was sad, my sadness began to lift. My sadness eased up just through acknowledging my truth, rather than continuing to exert my energy trying to resist that I was sad. The saying "what we resist persists" is the truth. When I was resisting my sadness, I was wasting my energy trying to pretend I felt differently. When I gave into my truth of being sad, I was able to sit with what was actually bothering me. As I gave myself this time to sit in my truth, rather than trying to cover it up, I was able to uncover my inner voice, which had been buried for so long.

My truth was that I was scared to death to allow people to see the real me. My sadness helped me to address that fear. My sadness told me it was not worth letting go of my true self in order to try to please others, as I was miserable. The truth was that even though I tried so hard to be everything to everyone, I felt like I was still disappointing them most of the time. Through embracing my feelings, I realized that since I already felt like I was disappointing others as I tried to please them, I could not be much worse of a disappointment if I was actually myself. By listening to the wisdom that was present in my emotions, I slowly began to allow myself to be me. The more I was myself, the happier I was and the more my sadness diminished. When I fell back into trying to please or accommodate others, my sadness reappeared.

After years of sadness permeating my life, I am glad to say that I now rarely feel sad. Because I am connected to my Spirit and my truth, the majority of my life feels happy. However, when sadness comes to me, I no longer fight this feeling. I am able to welcome my sadness because I know this feeling will bring me closer to living from my truth.

Now when I feel sad, a special feeling comes over me. My sadness is a gift to me because it slows me down. As I slow down, it becomes a time of honoring myself. I nurture and respect my Spirit even more, as I am being given a feeling telling me to slow down and listen. When I am slowed down, I am able to better examine if there is an aspect of my life that I could be handling differently that would bring me more peace, satisfaction, and joy. My sadness is there to awaken me and tell me there is more I need to acknowledge or pay attention to that is not in balance with the way I desire to live. Because I honor this feeling, I am able to understand with much more ease what is not in balance and what I need to do to create change. As soon as I make that change, my sadness is lifted and I feel happy and carefree again. It is quite beautiful.

Looking back, what has changed for me in order to embrace my sadness is that I do not blame or beat myself up any longer when my life is imbalanced. My sadness used to feel like a personal attack that reiterated to me that I was not enough or could not do things right. Now instead of seeing inadequacy, I see my sadness as a barometer helping me to further create the life I desire to live. Our sadness is a gift, because if we listen to what we feel sad about, we will be given the key to living a more peaceful and joyful life.

Now when I feel sad, I feel grateful. I feel grateful that I am being shown a new way if I allow myself to listen to my truth, my inner voice. I also feel grateful that through listening to my inner voice, I have dramatically changed my life. When I become sad now, it is not the overwhelming sense of sadness I used to feel. If I feel overwhelmed in sadness, the feeling is very temporary, because I am able to recognize my truth with greater ease. My truth is no longer buried within me, it is simply right below the surface. I feel grateful that I am able to access this wisdom and guidance in order to create further changes that will support me in living my best life. Even if this guidance at times has to demonstrate to me that my actions in the past were not for my highest good, I have learned to open myself to listen. I may not want to see how I was not living my best life, yet as I do, I am ensured that I am able to create changes that will support me to live life feeling more fulfilled.

In my sadness, I feel loved, because I know that I am being shown the way to becoming further aligned toward my heart's desires. I give thanks for how much my sadness has helped me create necessary shifts. I also give thanks that my life is so dramatically different than it used to be. My life now seems like a dream, as I allow my inner voice to guide me, leading me to new and exciting experiences I never would have thought possible in the past. This is all possible because my sadness led me back to my truth, and my truth always leads me to happiness.

Whenever we feel sad, we need to embrace that sense of emptiness we feel internally. We feel empty because we are utilizing people and objects external to ourselves in order to fill ourselves and our sense of worth. By allowing ourselves to sit with our feelings of emptiness and sadness, our truth emerges and we begin to find meaning in our lives. This meaning is significant, as it comes authentically from us rather than through others' sense of what is important. Rather than feeling sadness and emptiness, we feel whole again by living authentically in our truth. We can all choose to create unimaginable blissful living when we choose to listen to our truth. From our sadness, our truth is revealed. May we all choose to listen intently and carefully to how our Spirit is guiding us in order that we may know the gift of truly living.

Recognizing Our Arrogance in Order That We Live More Compassionately

When I am able to recognize that I am acting arrogantly, I feel ashamed. I feel ashamed that I am not a better human being. I feel that I should be beyond being arrogant, especially if I am to teach being aligned with our truth and Spirit. My truth, however, is that at times I am arrogant, and because I am, I need to be compassionate toward myself, as this is a part of me.

Although a part of me feels embarrassed that I can still be arrogant at times, I am grateful for this latest experience. I have been feeling the need to gain more compassion in my life, and believe it or not, my arrogance is granting me that wish. When I become arrogant and begin talking too much about myself or making myself feel very important, it is because I am not feeling seen, valued, or admired. Through my arrogance, I see that what I am actually trying to do is show or prove to others that I am special or have qualities that should make me be liked or accepted. The only reason I would need to do this is because at that particular moment, I am not feeling that who I am is enough for others to accept or like. When the old fear that I am not enough becomes triggered, my ego kicks in, trying to demonstrate how I am likeable or enough.

Rather than coming across as likeable, however, I am seen as "full of myself," which pushes people away from me. The truth is at that moment, I am trying to fill myself with external "proof" that I am good, because inside I feel empty.

My sense of emptiness only occurs when I believe in the lie that I am not enough. Thus, because my underlying belief is that I do not feel special, I create a scenario in which I feel bad about myself. Instead of feeling liked by others, which is what I truly desired, my underlying beliefs about myself further separated me from people.

I am humbled that at times my ego still grabs a hold of me, so desperately wanting attention and love. I feel saddened for my Spirit, because I still do not always know my truth. Once I am able to come to terms with my truth, I feel grateful, because I know this is what it is like to be human. This is what keeps me connected to understanding why we do the things we do. Our actions are not always the most attractive, but underneath our behaviors, we just want to be loved for who we are. Our behaviors will attempt to create the love and acceptance we desire if we are not giving them to ourselves.

Seeing my arrogance, I now must ask myself, "Have I been acknowledging and loving myself?" Sadly, the answer is no. If I had been paying attention to my need to treat myself with love, care, and consideration, I would not need to have my needs externally validated. I have been so focused on the external, my goal to complete this book, that I have been ignoring my needs. My feelings have wanted me to take time for myself, to rest and relax. My Spirit has been calling me not to forget about myself as I delve into my work. Even though I am extremely passionate about this book, my Spirit is there to remind me that I cannot forget to nurture my soul. Without this self-nurturance, I forget that I am special and full of love, not because of what I do but just because I am. I am a spiritual being needing spiritual care to fuel myself internally. If I deplete myself internally, I am weakening my Spirit. As my Spirit weakens, my ego takes over and attempts to get my needs fulfilled from the external.

My arrogance is returning me to my truth. My arrogance is created from not feeling special because internally I have lost that understanding. I move from being ashamed to having compassion for myself getting so caught up in my goals and my life that I have forgotten about the essence of my existence. This essence is my Spirit, for without it, I would not be truly living.

I am grateful that through being able to recognize that I was not feeling like myself, I was able to make a shift. Because being arrogant is not my typical behavior, I could see that there was something off within me. I had to pay attention to my feelings, which always give me the information I need to make the appropriate adjustments. My arrogance was an invitation to bring me back to listening to what was going on with my soul. All my soul wanted was some tender loving care. My soul was calling for some yoga, a bath, and a walk in nature. Once I did, I was reconnected to my Spirit. The feelings of being ashamed for my actions vanished and I felt like me again, as I could recognize the beautiful, loving person that I am. Once I was able to recognize this for myself, there was no longer a need for me to try to have others recognize it within me. Thus, my arrogance vanished!

The Gift of All of Our Emotions

Through this examination of our different feelings, we can see that we are given a spectrum of emotions in order for us to support ourselves to recreate balance in our life. Although not every emotion could be covered in this chapter, the most common were examined in order for us to be able to recognize the traps most of us fall into when we choose not to address our feelings. Regardless of whether the emotions we have were discussed or not, we can apply the same method to understanding all of our feelings.

None of our emotions needs to be considered as bad–they are simply tools for us to utilize to help us recognize our truth. Our truth is that whatever we fear about our emotions - we are actually creating these types of experiences in not accepting and honoring our feelings. We fear our sadness because we fear feeling empty, yet we are indeed empty inside when we ignore this truth. We fear our anger because we do not like being out of control, yet we are out of control when we do not responsibly own our power. Uncovering our thoughts, feelings, and beliefs will benefit us toward being able to manifest the opposite of what we fear.

We limit our ability to manifest our heart's desires when a part of us is buying into a lie that leads us to living a majority of our lives with less-than-optimal feelings. Even though we are meant to experience pain, we do not need to make ourselves suffer. Suffering is elongated pain. We see that we can choose to take away the suffering by listening and honoring our pain.

Through our emotions, we can understand where we are imbalanced in order to create the change that will lead us to the optimal living state that we are all meant to be living. By being able to continue to create optimal living conditions within our psyche and Spirit, our energy is freed to focus on all the abundance we desire rather than attempting to push down that which we fear.

Putting this Chapter into Practice:
1) Now is your time to put yourself, your life, in a movie. Distance yourself from your ego and see how ridiculous it is how often and how much you torture yourself. This is cruelty. Now choose a new movie to watch, one in which you listen to your feelings and follow your inner guidance with ease. What type of adventures is your life taking you on now?
2) A natural way to support your emotional shifts is to utilize flower essences. Flower essences are the energetic imprint of flowers. Each flower has a unique imprint that can support your emotional functioning. The impact is subtle at first, as it takes times to recognize the impact. I have used flower essences for years and cannot imagine beginning my

day without them. For more information about flower
essences and their use, go to www.flowersociety.org
or www.edwardbach.org.

Chapter 6
Understanding Our Life as a Part of a Continuum

Seeing our emotions as a spectrum in which we are given the opportunity to experience both that which feels good as well as that which feels bad to us is a gift. We are given this spectrum in order that we can make shifts from less-than-optimal living to optimal living states of being. Of course, the different components and/or experiences that comprise our lives can sometimes make staying in an optimal living state challenging. This is a natural part of the ebb and flow of the Universe. At times, life will feel effortless and easy because we are in complete synchronicity with the Universe. Other times we may feel more challenged because we are being given the opportunity for further growth. Through our growth, we are more able to receive spiritual, physical, and emotional abundance in our lives. This ebb and flow is part of the continuum of our spiritual growth on this human plane that offers us the gift of experience in order that we are impacted from the depths of our souls. As our souls are impacted, we move further along the continuum on our Spirit's journey to living freely.

Understanding the Continuum Concept

In Western society, we tend to try to label everything–events, objects, people, and actions. Categorizing life in this way appears to help people make more sense of our world. The problem is that when we label or categorize, we can actually be limiting our understanding of the truth. Categorization, especially when it comes to either-or labeling, is inaccurate, because this only describes two opposite ends of the spectrum. The truth is that most of us tend to be somewhere in between. It is more accurate to perceive ourselves as part of a continuum between two states in which our energy fluctuates.

Continuum thinking is open and allows for fluidity, while categorizing or labeling tends to be restrictive. Think of all that we label that is not accurate. We attempt to categorize people into being Democrat or Republican, homosexual or heterosexual, white or black, etc., as if there are no other options. As our world changes, we can see that this limited thinking does not work for most people anymore. Yet we still attempt to label because we have not opened ourselves to be receptive to other options.

The point of discussing the concept of continuums is because it impacts our perceptions of life. Our perceptions need to be in connection with the truth in order for us to be able to live the life we are intended to live. We will feel more supported to live the life we are intended to live when we can recognize the fluidness of our reality. Because we are energetic beings, we are in a constant state of flux. Our energy shifts without us even being able to perceive it at times. As we strive for being in our truth, having faith, and trusting in God, our ability to do so will fluctuate. What we are trying to do is live in those states that are most desirable for us with more consistency. We want to live toward finding the right shift in the continuum that brings us peace, happiness, and passion for living.

As our states of being shift away from our desires, we are being supported to move past our comfort zone to progress closer toward our dream. Even though we may take a few steps backward, this is not bad. It may not feel great at the time, yet we need to step back once in a while to gain deeper understanding and perspective. Through gaining a broader perspective, we are able to move forward even further toward feeling in alignment with our truth.

Recognizing Our Shifts on the Continuum of Faith

In order to further understand the concept of how we shift on a continuum, let us use faith as an example. If we have a period of time when we lose faith, this does not mean that we have lost our dream. First, if we are able to recognize that our faith has lessened, even plummeted, we are in a good place, because we are aware. This means we have moved from a place of being less conscious of our feelings to being very aware. We need to honor our awareness, because living consciously is integral to creating the life we desire. We can recognize that although our faith has lessened, we have still created shifts on the continuum from living life unconsciously to living more consciously. Even though our faith may have been depleted temporarily, it is temporary.

Losing faith happens when there is a block within us that needs to be addressed in order for us to gain deeper faith in what we believe. Losing faith helps us attain a deeper understanding of how losing our connection with our truth does not serve us. If we allow ourselves to take in what we are supposed to learn, we will gain further clarity, which will support our faith. Our faith becomes stronger in order for us to be able to withstand the periods in our lives in which we will need faith to manifest our desires.

Seeing ourselves as part of a continuum rather than categorizing and labeling ourselves as either this or that is a much more gentle way to view ourselves and others. When we categorize, there is no room for "mistakes." If we are to make a "mistake," suddenly we are a part of a different category. In one action, we went from seeing ourselves as a person with the qualities we desire to a person without those qualities. When we perceive ourselves on a continuum, we can more accurately recognize our energy flows, our dips, and our surges. In essence, we are able to see our truth without critiquing ourselves, or at least hopefully with less judgment.

Remember, Jesus Christ, too, questioned, doubted, and lost faith. Nevertheless, we never thought of him as someone without faith. There is room for us to question, doubt, and lose faith. We can shift on the continuum because when we do, we will bounce back with further strength. God intended for us to have our swings on the continuum in order to grow to more consistently being in the state we want to live.

There Is a Simple Question that Allows Us to Make Shifts

When we question and even doubt, we are actually freeing ourselves up to receive the answers we need. What will serve us better, though, is to be clear about our questioning. Even shifting our questioning from "why?" to "how?" will give us greater support. When we ask "how," we are more open to receiving guidance. When we ask "why," we are fighting what is. "Why" suggests a struggle with the wisdom of the Universe, which equates to losing faith. "How," on the other hand, states that we have faith yet we need support. The support that we are then given is provided to demonstrate that we are far more capable than we give ourselves credit for.

When we are willing to adopt asking how instead of why, we believe that we will get the support we need. We remember we are indeed powerful in knowing that we can ask for support, receive it, and act accordingly. Because we know that we are always being cared for by the Universe, we lose faith less and less. In other words, we are moving on the continuum from pain to greater peace. We want to move from experiencing pain deeply and often to experiencing pain less and with less severity. We will experience pain less severely when we spend less time feeling like a victim of life, asking, "Why me?" By instead asking, "How can you help me make it through this experience?" or "What is it you need me to learn from this experience?" we will feel more empowered to take action toward creating change.

As we adopt God and the Universe as our support, we will naturally move on the continuum from living life mostly out of fear to mostly from love. For most of us, even when we are living our life with love, we will still have times or circumstances in which we react out of fear. This is part of being human. We are then given the opportunity to recognize our fear in order to further our alignment with love.

There Is a Learning Curve that Occurs before We Shift

By recognizing that we are always supported, we are less fearful of what life has to offer. Even when life does not go according to our plan, we will see room for opportunity rather than just pain. Allowing ourselves to trust in the guidance we will be given ultimately strengthens our faith and the love we feel toward life. As our faith strengthens, our perception of the dichotomy between our notions of heaven and Earth changes to recognizing that heaven can be on Earth if we allow it to be. It is just a matter of degree and time until we create that reality.

As we embark on the journey of moving from fear to love, realize that we will be given many experiences to challenge us. We are given these experiences in order to be certain that we are truly ready to take the necessary actions that we need to make. For instance, let's say that we feel we need to become more assertive with ourselves and stop acting like a doormat. The Universe will then inundate us with numerous instances in which we are confronted to fall into the pattern of being a doormat. At first, we are likely taken off guard and remain the doormat a few times. Even though our actions have not yet shifted, we still have changed. We are now bitterly aware of how much this pains us. In fact, we become so angry that we are willing to change. The next few times we will actually stand up for ourselves. We may also be a bit overly dramatic about it as well, because we are new at this. This is okay. This will be part of our learning curve.

The good news is that the Universe will continue to set up conditions in which we will have the option to fall into our old behavior, which does not serve our highest good, or to choose exerting our truth, which does. As we get down pat how we would like to assert ourselves, the lessons will lessen. Nevertheless, as we will see in the following example, the Universe will still throw in some tests, even after we have gotten good at our new behavior, just to make sure we do not unconsciously fall back into an old pattern.

A Recent Shift on My Continuum of Spiritual Growth

All this spiritual growth and still my mother can get to me! I am not sure if I am angrier with her or myself because I did not speak my truth. Now that I hear myself, I know that my anger is toward me because I did not confront her with my truth. It was an instance in which my mother was criticizing my children's behavior while we were out to eat at a restaurant. Actually, it was really my behavior she was criticizing, because she thought I should have better control of them.   She couched her criticism by saying something like, "I am not saying this to be critical." Instead of being in my truth and sharing how her judgment was making me feel, I just shook my head and meekly said, "Oh, I know."

When I am not in my truth, I recognize it very easily and am able to understand the core of the matter. It is not the fact that my Mom criticized my kids that angered me. I am upset for going back to an old pattern of not wanting to cause waves. My truth knows that. Allowing me to experience not standing up for myself again is good, because I am reminded that it does not feel good or right to me.

Through having experiences in which I feel bad for not being in my truth, I feel more of a need to be in my truth at all times. Having enough of these experiences allows me to stay aware of my tendency to go back to patterns that do not serve my highest good. By being more aware, I will be able to catch myself before falling back into my old behavioral patterns of not wanting to share my truth. My pain reminded me again that I must be conscious of my tendencies and who makes me the most vulnerable to sway from my truth. Recognizing my tendencies will support me to make changes in those areas so that I continue on my path of living from my truth.

When instances like these occur in our lives in which we notice we were not in our truth after the fact, we may wonder what to do. At those times, we need to go within ourselves and listen to our inner voice. In my case, my Spirit told me to do nothing. I was to wait for it to occur again and then give thanks that I am given another opportunity to discuss from my heart how this makes me feel. If an experience is weighing on our heart, then our Spirit may direct us to address the issue right away. We must be attuned to ourselves to listen for what is best in each instance.

Regardless of when our Spirit directs us to address the matter, our Spirit wants us to recognize the point of being in our truth. Sharing our truth is imperative for creating balance, not only in our lives but for those who hurt us as well. Not only do we need to recognize how it feels to not share our truth, the other person/s involved need to at least be aware that their words or actions have impacted us. By sharing our truth and therefore giving them this information, we are providing them with an opportunity as well to rebalance and create integral shifts for both of us.

When we reclaim our power by being in our truth, we are giving ourselves and those who were involved in our pain a gift. Even if they do not take our truth as a gift, know inside that it is. Just as my mom's words were a gift to me to help me recognize that I need to own up to my power even more than I am currently, so will the truth be to help her live from her highest self.

Look at how different our notion of confrontation would look if we addressed it from a loving place. Coming from my heart, I am not worried about how the situation will turn out. I have trust that when it comes from my heart, I am aligned with all that is good and good will come out of the situation. The experience taught me that it was still my initial reaction to react out of fear. There is still a part within me that wants to please my Mom and get her validation. Yet when I am seeking validation outside myself, I loose my truth. Is this always the case? No, but this experience demonstrated to me that there is still room for me to go deeper and explore why I am more easily triggered in certain circumstances. As I address this, I create further alignment with my highest self.

This experience with my Mom helped me to become more aware of how I am not in alignment with my highest self as well as how to approach these types of scenarios through love rather than the fear that I am not enough. I am grateful, because I know that I will move again on the continuum closer to living more fully from love and further away from fear. When we are in fear, we take experiences personally. When we feel love, we are able to understand the gifts in all that we are given. I give thanks that many of my gifts of growth are now manageable to me, as I can now address and understand them with minimal pain.

As it turns out, my Mom recognized for herself that her words were hurtful and called right away to apologize. As she did, I admitted that I was hurt and then let it go. I honored the fact that our relationship has changed enough for her to now recognize without me telling her that I have been hurt and that she willingly apologized. Initially we both fell into an old pattern, but because that pattern is not typical in our relationship anymore, she was able to recognize with ease that her comments did not feel good to herself or me. I was easily able to be in my truth, forgive, and forget, because I know that our relationship has now shifted to being defined by respect rather than criticism.

I give thanks to my mother for this experience because I know I need further practice with this skill. Having this skill of remaining in my truth will keep me being upfront and honest in all circumstances, especially when I feel uncomfortable doing so. I recognize that I will likely need this skill in order to talk to others about my work. I thank the Universe for the support I am granted in steps that I can handle, and take in, and I resolve to do better for myself and my highest good. I am loved and I am grateful for the experiences that prepare me to further own my full power!

We Choose People and Experiences to Support Us to Create Shifts in Our Continuum toward Optimal Living

As mentioned in Chapter 3, the experiences that we encounter are there for us to support us to attain living to our highest potential. In order for this to occur, we choose or even create experiences that will support us to make necessary changes in our life. My belief is that prior to be incarnated in this lifetime, there were certain experiences that we agreed to as a means of creating shifts toward becoming more aware of the truth of our Spirit. Many times these are the life-altering experiences we have all had, regardless if we label those experiences as "good" or "bad."

Along with these experiences, we also choose people who will be our supporters and teachers. These people ensure that we get what we need to in order to continue moving on our continuum toward our highest spiritual development. We choose people who will offer us the necessary support we need when we lose faith in ourselves and life. These people may not even be blood related, yet we will feel a certain connection with them instantaneously.

One of my special connections is with my Nana. My Nana had no biological connection to me, as she was my cousin's grandmother, yet we were meant to be together. My Nana saw goodness in me always and gave me the gift of unconditional love. To her, I was the little girl in her life she never had. Even though she is no longer on Earth physically, I still feel her presence with me. She is still the shoulder I cry on when I feel afraid or worn out in life.

My son Jonah has this special connection with my Dad. It is amazing to witness how even at a very young age, Jonah has been drawn to my Dad, almost to the point of obsession when he sees him. Whenever my Dad comes for a visit, he cannot put Jonah down. This started when Jonah was only a few months old, and their bond continues. Also interesting is that Jonah's middle name, Walter, is my Dad's first name. Jonah must have told me even while he was in my womb that he was to have a part of my Dad connected to him. Jonah was the one I chose to receive my Dad's name rather than Jonah's twin brother.

The idea of "soul mates" is exactly this type of connection. Our soul mates are the ones we have chosen because they are the ones who will support us in reaching our highest spiritual potential. This is why couples often feel that in just a short time, they have known each other much longer. Oftentimes it is because they have, just in different lifetimes.

What may be difficult to realize is that the relationships that are challenging to us are also people we have signed up with to provide us valuable teachings. These are some of the most significant agreements we have made in order to provide us with experiences to help us grow to who we are supposed to be. These relationships are just as sacred as those people who have provided us support. Our tumultuous relationships make "sacrifices" from a spiritual perspective in order to create the necessary experiences of our lives. Through these experiences, our sense of self becomes shaped. Whenever we are shaped by another, regardless if we label how they impacted us as good or bad, this is in connection with a part of our purpose.

Imagine from the spiritual plane that before any of the significant people in our lives were born and long before we were conceived, we made certain agreements with these Spirits. These Spirits have agreed to provide us with specific experiences in order to elicit the spiritual growth we want to experience while living in the human form. Some Spirits will agree to incarnate in order to be very difficult to get along with in our lives. Maybe that person agreed to be emotionally or physically abusive in order for us to become the person we are. If we dare to look at these people from a spiritual level, we will be able to recognize that because of their love for us, they will be willing to be an ass or even worse in order that we may grow and move on the continuum of our spiritual growth. By them having that experience, they will also learn important teachings that will support their movement on the continuum toward their own development as well.

Having this perspective toward those who have hurt and even abused me has helped me to let go of my anger and hurt toward their actions. Even though they provided me with painful experiences, I am able to recognize how those experiences impacted me in the long run. Even though for many years those experiences devastated me, the pain that I was caused shaped me to desire a deeper understanding of the human healing process. These experiences, although painful, created my passion! Having gone through those experiences has taught me my strength along with many other specific teachings. I give thanks that I have learned the lessons I did in order to become the person I am. Would I ever want to go through those experiences again? Heck no! From my human perspective, I would never choose that for myself or anyone. However, from a spiritual perspective, I can understand why I had to.

We also manifest experiences, which may not be pleasant, through our day-to-day living based on our souls' need for us to change. One of my past manifestations was a peptic ulcer. I literally chuckled to myself once I realized that I had manifested this pain within me. I saw humor not because I did not take my ulcer seriously. I did. I laughed because I recognized instantaneously why I manifested this ulcer.

For quite a while, I have been receiving guidance to clean up my nutritional habits. I knew my Spirit wanted me to give up caffeine, alcohol, and sugar, but with three young kids, I relied on those addictions as crutches to help me unwind or give me more energy. I thought, "Maybe when my children are older, I will be able to focus more on what I am putting into my body, but right now it is too tough!" After all, my caffeine and alcohol consumption were quite minimal compared to our society's norm. Intuitively, though, I kept getting nudges that my body needed better nutrition, but I would not listen for long. Thus, I developed an ulcer.

My ulcer has been a gift, because it made me clean up my nutritional act quickly. Since my ulcer, I must be even more cognizant about what I am putting into my body and the impact it has on me. I notice how much better I feel when I fuel myself with nutritious food and beverages. More important, I feel the impact on my Spirit. This is what my Spirit wanted me to experience. I am amazed at how much better I am feeling emotionally, spiritually, and physically based on what I am and am not consuming. For instance, just letting go of the need for caffeine has allowed me to feel more attuned to what my body really needs to be nourished. The impact is greater than I imagined!

Would I have chosen to give myself an ulcer or even to eliminate or diminish certain foods and beverages that I enjoy? Absolutely not; from my human perspective, they were a part of typical daily living. My spiritual perspective, however, made me laugh and recognize how my Spirit will manifest for me experiences in order to force me to create the necessary changes that from a spiritual level I crave. In fact, my Spirit finds more of a need to create experiences for me when I do not desire them for myself. For this and all the experiences my Spirit has created in order to nudge me along on my continuum of growth, I am grateful and feel immensely blessed.

It is important to note that if I dismissed the message my Spirit was trying to give me through my ulcer by not changing, my Spirit would have needed to do more to get my attention. Another choice I had was to treat my symptoms through medications, while continuing to maintain more or less my same dietary habits. If that were the case, I am certain that I would have had to develop even further physical problems as a means to ensure that my habits would change once and for all.

As it turns out, I did not get the entirety of the message with my ulcer: I needed to take more drastic measures. Even though the ulcer went away, having my cervical dysplasia reappear, as mentioned in Chapter 3, has given me further guidance toward cleaning up my nutritional act.

Honoring Ourselves Creates Less Dramatic Shifts

Our willingness to listen to our inner voice and the guidance we are receiving will create less of a need for us to manifest painful experiences or bring unpleasant people into our lives. When we listen to our guidance, we will be able to move in the direction we desire on our continuum of spiritual growth. If we choose not to listen, we must recognize that our Spirit will continue amplifying our pain in order to get our attention.

Other times, we may not get the message as fully as we are intended to. In those cases, we will be given another opportunity to create the change the Universe is asking us to make. For instance, my ulcer was an initial message about my eating habits. Although I made some significant shifts, there was more I needed to do in order to feel my best. Of course, I would not make these shifts voluntarily, and therefore the dysplasia occurred as a means to make me be willing to do more.

Even though we will still have challenging moments in our day-to-day living, for the most part, these shifts will be less dramatic. We will still "mess up" at times and move in a direction that does not feel good to us. The difference is that it will become easier each time we take a step back to move forward again. Having these experiences supports us to move through a challenging issue much more quickly, because we have gained faith through our past experiences that we can find our way back to living optimally. Recognizing and honoring these subtle shifts will allow us to live life more freely. Living freely means that we are able to honor our shifts without judgment toward ourselves. Oftentimes I still have to remind myself that even though I am living from my truth does not mean that I will not sway from my truth. I am not perfect, and at times I will still be guided by my fears. Yet as this occurs, I allow myself to feel my emotions, which tell me that my actions, thoughts, or beliefs were not in congruence with my highest self.

Yesterday I had one of those moments with my kids in which I felt incredibly powerless to have them stop crying. Typically I am pretty tolerant of their feelings, yet yesterday I was feeling tired myself. At the same time, one of my sons was having an extremely sensitive day. I could not leave his side without him getting upset. This does not bode well when I have two other young children who need me as well. What happened? I was tolerant for a while and then I lost it. I could not take the screaming and started screaming myself! Usually I understand that my screaming only escalates the behavior that I am trying to have subside. At that moment, though, I felt powerless. When we feel powerless, we get angry and frustrated. Once I was able to recognize that I could positively impact my children once I reclaimed my power by being calm and loving again, I did.

Afterward I was sad that I had started yelling back at my kids. Through honoring my feelings, however, I was able to gain compassion for myself. This was not my typical behavior, and there is room for me to move from living from my ideal. When I move myself away from my ideal, I am given an opportunity to recognize why it is worth the extra effort and energy I put toward creating the life I desire. Thus, this experience reiterates my need to care for myself, because when I am depleted, I cannot give my best. I also gain deeper compassion for all of us as we face challenges. Sometimes we will be able to handle them gracefully and other times less so, yet all experiences are there to support us to live our best life.

In certain aspects of our lives, we may feel more challenged to move in the direction that we desire on our continuum. Furthermore, the energy we desire to put toward certain aspects of our lives will change the further we grow. Maintaining the appropriate balance while we spiritually grow as humans is why there is an ebb and flow to our lives. May we honor and have compassion for every movement we make on our continuum of spiritual growth. In seeing the blessing in every direction that we take, we will find more peace and enjoyment in our living.

Putting this Chapter into Practice:
1) Begin to observe your own movements on the continuum of creating your optimal life. Either mentally or in a journal, acknowledge when you created a shift toward your ideal. Whether it is choosing a healthier meal or not reacting out of your ego, notice the instances, either in the moment or in your recent past, when you chose differently than your typical reaction. Celebrate those moments and yourself for each small shift, as you will find how quickly they add up to creating your ideal.
2) Acknowledge right now the shifts that you know deep down inside that your Spirit would like you to currently make. You do not have to choose to make those shifts right now. Simply ask how you can gently be supported to create change that will get you closer to that ideal. Sometimes we can get caught up into "all-or-nothing" thinking that prohibits us from making any movement. Our Spirit honors even the small movements we create. A small movement may simply be the acknowledgment of the need for change, even if we are not yet willing to create a shift. As we

demonstrate our willingness to honor our inner guidance in small ways, we will be given further support as we eventually work toward our ideal.

Chapter 7
The Importance of Boundaries

Once we become used to asking for support and nurturing ourselves as we listen to the nudges our inner voice gives us, we are going to feel much more balanced, happier, and healthier in our living. The more we are able to maintain this balance, the stronger our inner voice will be. Balance creates the space for our inner voice to be heard, which increases our capacity to allow in our Spirit's guidance. In order to maintain the balance we have created within ourselves, as well as to prohibit further emotional and spiritual clutter from coming into our lives, we need to have healthy boundaries in place.

In order to have healthy boundaries, we must first know our inner truth. Our work throughout the first half of this book has allowed us to more clearly know our truth. Establishing healthy boundaries in our lives will support us to live more consistently from our truth. Having boundaries is not about having an indestructible wall that prevents anyone from connecting to us. Rather than perceiving boundaries as a wall, we are better served envisioning boundaries as a filter. Boundaries filter energy by blocking that which is not aligned with our Spirit. At the same time, our boundaries allow in energy that is best for our highest good. We envision this type of filter surrounding us at all times, creating energetic protection.

In order for our boundaries to work, we need to go beyond envisioning them. We also need to feel from the inside that we honor our Spirit and are willing to do what it asks of us. Our inner voice, which is coming from Spirit, will speak our truth if we allow it to. By allowing ourselves to be open with our truth, we will be energetically putting out to the world what we consider appropriate energy to come to us and energy that we do not find suitable for our highest good. Without listening to our truth and creating healthy boundaries, we are allowing in energy that is ill-suited for our hearts' desires.

Our Societal Disease of Lack of Healthy Boundaries

As a society, it appears as though we have lost a sense of having balance because so many of us no longer understand what it means to have appropriate boundaries. Stereotypically it has been women who have taken on the role of giving, while men tended to be too guarded. Today we can see both genders exhibiting boundaries that are either too rigid or too loose. Neither, however, serves us in living a joyful and peaceful life. Being too rigid or having no or little boundaries are perfect examples of being either too far left or too far right on the continuum of healthy boundaries. Healthy boundaries are right in the middle. In order to work toward creating healthy boundaries, we must address the blocks that have become so common that they are now problematic in our society.

Living With Overly Rigid Boundaries

Being overly rigid with our boundaries inhibits us from creating a life that feels good because those feelings are largely being blocked. Of course, guarded people can still have moments of happiness, but they are limited, because they feel they must be on the defensive most or all of the time. We become overly guarded when we've been hurt, usually by someone who meant a great deal to us. The people who hurt us were people we should have been able to trust with our feelings, but we learned the hard way we could not. Therefore, we took from those experiences that showing our true selves and our feelings equates to experiencing pain.

Because the pain that we felt was so hurtful, we learned to be constantly on guard, trying to ensure that others would not get away with hurting us again.

An example is not taking other people's comments as if they were personal attacks. When we feel balanced within, we are able to recognize when others may be inwardly struggling and we are able to let go of comments that may not be appropriate. However, if we have a hard time letting go, that is our internal clue that we are defending a wound that is still significant to us.

Whenever we are hyper-vigilant about any thought, we are bringing those experiences into our life. Again, this is the Law of Attraction, in which like attracts like. Hence, if our thoughts are about needing to protect ourselves from others because people are inherently bad or are out only for themselves, we will have those types of experiences. Because of these thoughts, we are also less likely to experience fun or joyful experiences because our perception of life is just the opposite. We are too busy trying to project ourselves as powerful or tough in order that others will not see through our wall, behind which we feel incredibly vulnerable.

All our protection keeps people exactly where we want them, away from us. We have created what we thought we desired, but our souls long for more. Our souls crave more laughter, greater connections with people, and to let go of all the pain we are holding onto in our lives. In order for our souls to be free, we must become willing to be vulnerable again and even experience pain.

Now that we are adults, we must trust that we will be able to address our pain. Furthermore, we have a greater opportunity to be wise about whom we choose to begin sharing our truth with. When we are young, we have limited options of who is in our life. As adults, we can choose to have supportive and loving people in our life or to utilize professional help in order for us to release our fears. Pain only lasts forever if we choose it to. When we are overly guarded, we are choosing living in fear of our pain over living the life we desire. By being willing to demonstrate our strength through sharing our truth, regardless of what those feelings are, we will no longer be a prisoner of the walls we put up around us.

Living with Few or No Boundaries

By far the most common block that I witness is the struggle with a lack of boundaries. This occurs when we allow people to take advantage of us or we typically end up doing more than we truly desire. Our giving is considered overly extensive because we end up depleted, exhausted, and run down, as we have no energy left within ourselves. Furthermore, we tend to feel that we give and give and then are treated poorly by others. We then wonder why this occurs.

Have you been the person making invitations over and over again to go out with you or come over, and do not get a response? Do you feel you bend over backwards in a friendship or relationship, whether personal or work related, yet you do not receive the same type of treatment in return? Are you constantly feeling like you are running yourself ragged? If you answered yes to any of these questions, you are likely struggling with not having appropriate boundaries.

When we overly give, we are not allowing the space for others to give back. Therefore, if we choose to give to the extent to which we feel overwhelmed, put out, or in pain, we have created an imbalance in those relationships. In giving to the degree that we do not feel good, we set it up for others not to treat us well. In fact, there is no room for others to treat us well, since we are doing all of the giving.

When we take on the role of the giver, there is no room for us to receive, because it will never be enough for us. Other people will never be able to give back to the degree that we have given because our giving is so out of balance. Nevertheless, we feel they should be giving back more than they are due to our imbalanced sense of giving. We end up feeling taken for granted and empty inside. They give up and walk away feeling freed from the burden of trying to match filling our needs.

Our needs become out of balance and too much for others to handle when we are not taking care of ourselves. Yet we cannot take care of our own needs when we are too busy taking care of everyone else's. We tend to become resentful toward everyone else because they are not willing to give as much as we have given to them. Hence, when we overly give, we set it up so others cannot win. No matter what they give, it will not feel like enough because we have given too much.

When we give and others do not reciprocate, we of course want to blame them. The truth is that this really is our own fault. No one asked us to give to the degree that leaves us feeling depleted. We did that to ourselves. Even if someone did ask, we have the responsibility to ourselves and our families to say no. It is our responsibility to have appropriate boundaries in order that we have the energy to give to those we are truly responsible for in our lives. Others are benefited when we have true, authentic energy to give rather than giving out of a sense of obligation.

The Underlying Truth to Our Excessive Giving

Why then do so many of us tend to overly give? We do this because it fills our own need to feel needed so that we do not feel so empty inside. Being needed gives us a sense of worth. If we do not feel worthy, we come up with ways to be needed in order to have our own needs met. By doing all this giving, we feel altruistic. Others pull back even though we are giving because they can energetically feel there are ties attached to our giving. The unspoken tie is that others are to make us feel good about ourselves when we give to them. Although we are "giving," we are really only doing so to have our own need met for feeling of worth and value.

We are energetic beings who are able to sense the meaning behind people's actions. We recognize internally on some level whether someone is giving out of a desire to give or if they are doing so in order to feel better about themselves. It comes across in our energy.

What is most unfortunate is that people who are giving in order to have their needs met are not able to recognize it. They give so much because they are "trying to be nice" or "a good person." If we feel like we are giving much more than we are receiving in our friendships or relationships, then we are. Instead of others gravitating to us for being nice, they pull back. People pull away because energetically they feel manipulated, since they can "read" in our energy that our giving is not based on a desire to give but instead is an obligation. The obligation is to either have our own needs met to feel valued and worthy or to soothe our guilt. Neither of those options feels good to others on an energetic level. In order for us to stop bringing those types of experiences into our lives, we need to address our sense of boundaries.

The Good Girl Syndrome

Although men can also fall prey to being "too good", women are especially prone to falling into the trap of being "the good girl". What is interesting about "the good girl syndrome" is that we can be completely successful in one area of our life yet in another area we succumb to being the good girl. In other words, the good girl is not about being a people pleaser or doormat; it is much more subtle. This is why so many people find themselves stuck because they are trying to remain the good girl.

The adult version of the good girl syndrome includes the following: (1) when we say yes when we really want to say no; (2) when our feelings get hurt yet we do not say a word; or (3) we completely disagree but we go along with it anyway. The good girl syndrome is interesting because it is what women in particular fall back to when they do not know their value in a relationship. For instance, maybe they have a great marriage yet they question their worth when it comes to their career. Perhaps it is the other way around where they have been greatly successful in their career yet they struggle with intimate relationships.

In those cases we are not certain of our worth, so we turn to others to have our worth validated. In order to receive that validation, we try to be the good girl. Why would we not? After all that is what we learned to do as children. We were told to get along and do not make waves in order to make those around us happier. Our rational minds bought into that if we can make others happy, we will be more liked, loved or admired.

Yet the good girl is not able to be truly happy if she is always stifling her essence. The good girl is not allowed to simply be. If we cannot be ourselves, there is no way we will ever feel true happiness let alone get what our hearts' truly desire. The truth of what we desire is masked by goodness of the good girl, and will forever stay that way until we are willing to share our true selves.

If you find yourself in a rut in a certain area of your life or continue to struggle with a certain person, examine if you have fallen victim of the good girl syndrome. Look at the difference between those areas of our lives in which we intrinsically know the value we bring versus this aspect in which we feel stuck. Notice the lack of certainty you have about you. Once you have a sense of certainty about who you are in all areas of your life, there will be no need to be the good girl. Your intrinsic goodness will shine through regardless if you disagree or disappoint another because you will know with certainty the truth of your essence. This can only occur by listening to your feelings and being willing to form boundaries in your life. If you are still curious as to how often you may be falling victim to being "the good girl," go to www.michellebersell.com and take my free quiz.

My Struggle with Creating Healthy Boundaries

One of the biggest areas where I needed to form boundaries was with my mom. Our lives were intermeshed to a point where it was not healthy for me because I had lost my identity. Reclaiming my identity was difficult for my Mom, because then she began to see that we were different in many ways. Reclaiming my voice meant sharing how I felt in our relationship, which was not always pleasant to hear. Of course, she was hurt and our conversations became challenging.

Being one of my greatest teachers, my Mom knew exactly which buttons to push that would typically get me to respond the way she wanted. My guilt would kick in that I was a bad person and an even worse daughter for sharing my feelings. Nevertheless, I began to opt to not allow my guilt to run me. I recognized that my guilt was not serving me, as I was truly unhappy listening to that voice. Furthermore, I saw how my guilt limited me from living the life I desired.

After these discussions with my Mom, a part of me would feel terrible for standing up for myself. Nevertheless, there was a bigger part of me that felt empowered and good because I was finally allowing myself to speak my truth. I chose to allow the part of me that felt good about those conversations to guide me. I could easily remember how I never felt good when I did not share my truth. What I found was that I could not share my thoughts and feelings when I was trying to be a "good daughter." By sharing my truth, I automatically began feeling better. I found that the more I stuck with sharing my true feelings, the better I felt and the easier it had become for me.

As I began to recognize my truth coming through me, the old beliefs about me and my life became dismantled. My fear was that if I was not a good daughter, my Mom would completely disconnect from me and I would no longer have her love. As I confronted this fear, I was able to recognize that my fear was a lie.

In order to confront my fear of no longer having my Mom in my life, I had to be willing to feel within myself that I would be okay should my fear come true. My fear was that

being myself would not be enough for her and I would not be
accepted into her life any longer. Although I knew it would
be painful to lose my Mom from my life, I knew that if I did
not stand up for myself in the relationship, my Spirit would
remain squandered.

As my Spirit grew stronger, one of the most important
ways I needed to change our relationship was to insist upon
respect in our conversations. To me that meant not being
yelled at or being called names. Of course, my Mom did not
like my ultimatum that I either am talked to with respect or
we do not talk at all. When the yelling and name calling
continued, I hung up the phone and my heart sank. My fear
was that we would not talk again. I also knew I had to be
willing to lose the relationship in order to be able for that fear
not to control me any longer. In other words, I had to surrender to my fear in order to be able to let go of the stranglehold
my fear had on me.

At this point in my life, I had felt so much pain for not
feeling loved for who I was that I was willing to be alone in
order to find internal peace. Because I was willing to live
without my mother's love, I was able to stand in my truth.
Being able to face my fear allowed me to create the relationship that I had always desired to have with her as an adult.
Although at times there was temporary separation between
us, in the long run we created a relationship based on mutual
respect and love. Through being in my truth, we became
closer. All along my fear told me that my truth would tear us
apart. My inner voice, however, knew exactly how to create
a healthier relationship with my mother in which both of us
would feel better about ourselves.

I share this story because I know that forming boundaries
can be very challenging to us emotionally. The reason we do
not have boundaries to begin with is due to a fear of not being
loved or being alone if we were to be in our truth. This fear
is very powerful. Yet we must recognize that if we do not
confront this fear, we will live with anger and sadness in our

hearts. Our hurt feelings will be because we have not formed boundaries with others in order to allow ourselves to live freely. Yes, boundaries are actually there to support us to be free to be ourselves. We need to remember to allow ourselves time and practice to own and speak our truth.

As mentioned previously, when we confront our fears within ourselves, the Universe will be there, supporting us by giving us plenty of opportunities to practice mastering our boundaries. Sometimes we will be great at forming new boundaries and other times we will not. All of these experiences are there to help us grow. In those instances where we do well, we need to take in how good it feels to establish boundaries with someone who in the past took advantage of or disrespected us. In those instances in which we chose not to be in our truth, we need to take in how that left us feeling upset. Thus, the Universe is reiterating to us how good it feels to speak our truth by giving us both experiences. Having both experiences actually helps our mind let go of the guilt as we are able to see how better off we are (and others are) when we live in our truth.

Creating Healthy Boundaries in Our Personal Relationships

When we feel that there is an imbalance in a relationship, it means the energy give-and-take is no longer in flow. Either we are giving too much and the other is not meeting that energy, or vice versa. The only way that relationship will work will be for the giver to pull back the energy being given away to that relationship. If the giver does not, that relationship will feel overwhelmed and burdened by an overwhelming sense of the need to give back an amount of energy that the other person does not have or is unwilling to give back.

A recent example of a relationship imbalance was when I was feeling disconnected from my best friend. Her life had become very busy due to her work, but it also seemed like there may have been something more causing the disconnection between us. I was beginning to no longer feel as important to her and her life, which was really hurtful to me. We talked about it a month earlier, and it felt good to share with her how I missed her. We promised to make more of a commitment to schedule regular talks in order to feel more connected again.

Our commitment to schedule our talks lasted for only a short time. We then fell back into a pattern in which I was calling her repeatedly and not getting much response or effort from her. Of course, I was taking this personally. After all, I was hurt and missed having these conversations with my best friend.

I was really feeling devastated by the potential loss of our friendship and was at a loss about what to do. Should I call her again and try to talk this out? Do I again tell her how hurtful this is to me? I was very upset, but something within me told me to wait and not call her.

I did not call her, and the next day we talked. I was guided to just listen to her. She talked about examples of her pulling back in her friendships. She was feeling like she was caretaking too much and was tired of putting so much effort toward her friendships. Other friends of hers were also feeling neglected because she was not returning their calls. Just listening to her, I felt more at peace, because I was able to recognize that this was not about me personally.

Being able to take a step back, I was able to gain some insight about her perspective. My friend was feeling overwhelmed by the energy she was exuding in her life. She was putting energy toward people who did not give it back to her in the same way. Although I was not one of those people, I recognized that when we are overwhelmed, the best thing to do is pull back in order to gain a better perspective. She did just that and began to let go of friends who were weighing her down rather than lifting her Spirit. In doing so, her time freed up again in order to give energy to the people whom she cared for and who cared for her as well.

By being able to step back and become the observer, I was able to acknowledge my friend's process. As I did, my hurt melted away, because I recognized that her process was not against me. Although her process may have caused me some hurt feelings, it was not about me. My pain was created in assuming that her lack of communication was directly related to her feelings toward me. By taking my ego out of the situation, I found the truth.

It is almost magical when we are able to come to terms with something causing us pain. Suddenly when we let go and find peace, the situation turns around by itself. I let go of trying so hard. Just as she was modeling to her friends that she wanted an equal energy exchange with them, I saw the same in our relationship. This is a perfect example how the people in our lives are our mirrors. In the case with my friend, it was up to me to pull back my energy. By correcting the amount of energy I was putting out in the friendship, we became rebalanced.

By pulling back some of the energy that I was putting toward the friendship, I was simply giving my friend the opportunity to come back into our relationship in what felt like a win-win for both of us. I was no longer upset with her because I was not giving my energy away to her and not getting it back in return. She no longer felt this burden to be there for me more than she could, which allowed and attracted her to come back to our friendship.

Let me further explain: if I am the one constantly calling her, she is always on the end of feeling responsible for returning my call. If, on the other hand, I recognize the imbalance in energy and temporarily stop calling her, I give her the opportunity to feel that she is giving to our friendship. Thus, instead of feeling like she is the one who needs to give, give, give in order to meet my or someone else's needs, she is able to act freely, because it is no longer an obligation. I then get to decide if the amount of energy she is willing to put into the relationship is a good match for me. If it is, our relationship will continue to grow. If it is not, I am able to look for the connection I desire with others instead of requiring her to change.

We also need to understand the difference between what we ultimately desire in relationships versus our short-term needs. My short-term need with my friend was to talk to her more often. My long-term desire, however, was to have a friendship in which there is mutual care, respect, and energy being exchanged. If I had just listened to my short-term needs, I would have kept calling her and been dissatisfied. Listening to my Spirit, on the other hand, I know that I am always being guided to create what is best for my highest good in the long run. What my Spirit was guiding me to do was have more inner reliance rather than needing my friend's validation for me to be in my truth. The Universe recognized how I was relying on my friend as a crutch to validate me was not for either of our greatest good. Because of my inner voice's guidance, I was able to let go of my short-term need and step back from our relationship in order to regain balance again. Thus, it is the voice of our Spirit that is our ultimate truth and that will lead us to all that we desire within ourselves and our relationships.

Through being in our truth, we allow the other person to take ownership of her actions and create her own sense of inner balance. Others can create their own sense of inner balance by sharing their truth, which may not be in alignment with ours, or they can change their behavior. We can then work together with those people in our lives to create the ideal circumstances for everyone involved. In other words, by being in our truth, we create the space for others to do the same. We also gain compassion when their truth is not in alignment with our own. Because we will have learned how good it feels to live in our truth, we will desire to continue creating scenarios in which everyone feels their best.

Creating Healthy Boundaries in Our Families

Because allowing ourselves and others to live in the truth benefits everyone, we must work to create energy exchanges in our families that feel good to everyone. One of the most significant areas in which boundaries often lapse is with our children and within our families. We already know that children need to have boundaries in order to prevent them from physically being harmed. For instance, we recognize the need for boundaries to prevent them from getting into poison or to be able to cross the street safely. We also need to be willing to provide boundaries for their spiritual and emotional well-being. We can do this by demonstrating how boundaries serve us toward creating the experiences we desire to have most often.

For my family's emotional and spiritual well being, I value peace. Peace does not mean quietness; rather, it means getting along. Peace also means being respectful of one another's needs. Creating peace in our family has taken a lot of effort, time, and energy. In fact, it is more or less a constant priority to teach and remind all of us how we can honor each other as well as ourselves. Nevertheless, I feel good that my kids are learning what it means to be respectful of others. In learning to be respectful of others, they are also learning that they have the right to have respect for themselves.

Too many parents are struggling in their homes because they have chosen not to create enough boundaries. Some parents are afraid of being "too mean" simply by having limitations or sharing how they feel with their kids. When we fear we are being "too mean" in these cases, we are allowing ourselves to be controlled by our fear of not being loved as much by our children if we are to assert boundaries.

There are also some parents who are just too tired to enforce their children's behavior. In not providing boundaries to our children, we teach them that it is okay to treat their parents (who are the people they love most) with disrespect.

In doing so, we are teaching them a lot on an emotional level about love.

Without boundaries, love means we can treat those we love the most disrespectfully. In addition, we become scared to be who we are for fear that those we love will not love us as much if we share our truth. How are we teaching them that if we are allowing them to do or say what they choose? They are learning from our actions, which reflect our fear that we cannot act in our truth. Furthermore, they are picking up on the lack of energy we are giving to them by not doing the more challenging job of creating and enforcing boundaries. If they are not worth our time and energy to support them to live their best life, they will feel less valued. They will then turn to the external to try to get their needs met of feeling worthy.

Since we all know how smart children are, we cannot doubt for a minute that they are not learning those lessons when boundaries are not in place. Is it any wonder then that we treat each other as we do when our concept regarding love is completely backward? The only way we can correct our children's concept of love is to correct this within ourselves. This is integral for our families, in order that we may model for our children the necessity of self-care and how that benefits others. We will correct our own concept of love by being willing to take care of our needs and speak our truth, as we create boundaries that will keep our families ultimately more joyful, playful, and at peace.

Important to remember is that each person's truth is unique. Therefore, there will be a difference in what one family's tolerance of behaviors are due to the unique circumstances of the individual makeup of each family member as well as the family unit as a whole. Although tolerance levels are variable, having clear boundaries establish a family environment that is for the best interests of everyone.

The Typical Struggle When Beginning to Form Boundaries

We need to be aware that when we form new boundaries, the people we are interacting with will likely protest. We may hear them calling us "mean," "selfish," or "conceited." The people who will interpret boundaries in this manner are doing so because they are upset that they can no longer get away with controlling or manipulating us. They used to be able to push us around, and now we have the audacity to say "Enough! I will not tolerate this any longer!" We need to understand that their reaction is normal, as they have been able to do something that benefitted them in the short term. Now, suddenly, they are being told to stop. Of course they will not like it, and they have an equally valuable point in sharing their feelings about our desired change.

We also must recognize that it may take some time in the relationship to rework how we interact. This will mean that we may have to continue to reinforce that we mean that we will no longer accept certain behaviors and be willing to demonstrate the consequences. In the short term, this is challenging, time-consuming work. The process takes away from our peace. In the long run, however, we are setting ourselves up for greater ease and less effort because what we are willing to accept is understood.

Parents recognize the initial challenge when they are enforcing a new rule with their children. At first, the rule is tested and fought with great hostility, yet when we are willing to demonstrate that what we say is our truth, our children begin to take in the boundaries we establish. If they want to be certain where we stand, they will continue to test us until they know what the boundary is that we require. By being able to believe in our truth and know it is for the betterment of all involved, we will be able to establish the foundation for the type of life we desire.

The problem that most often gets in the way of establishing boundaries is that most of us take other people's reactions personally. They will likely try to make it personal, yet it is really about them wanting to cross a boundary that does not feel right to our Spirit. We may feel a great surge of guilt afterward for enforcing our stance. We will feel guilty if we do not truly believe that our stance is for the betterment of everyone involved. If this is the case, we should not create the boundary until we know in our bones that it is right. The Universe will be there to continue to provide the pain we need until we are willing to understand that change needs to occur.

We may also experience guilt because it brings up our fears about standing up for ourselves. Our fear is that in standing up for ourselves, we are not respecting others. To address our guilt, we need to be able to decipher when we are standing up for ourselves due to our ego or if our Spirit is directing us. When our Spirit is directing us, we will know we are serving our best interests because we are coming from our heart and our truth. We will speak through our emotions and love. Furthermore, we are always being directed for the good of all those involved. Our ego, on the other hand, will be trying to serve our interests by trying to make ourselves feel right. When we confront our guilt and bring proof to our mind that the fears are not about our ego, we will start to gain more peace around forming boundaries.

Learning to Slow Ourselves Down in Order to Grow Emotionally

Learning to slow ourselves down is a key component to understanding our interactions with others. Oftentimes we react to people or situations rather than listening to what we are feeling throughout our experiences. This occurs most often when we do not like the experience we are having. If we do not like the experience, we are judging it and trying to move past it as quickly as possible. We have learned this from our past, when we were children and did not have many other options. We learned to "bite our tongue" or otherwise hide our emotions because we basically had to do so. If we did not, there were consequences.

Many of us stay frozen emotionally with regard to how we react to certain experiences and people. For this reason, a successful professional who is able to have calm interactions throughout her or his day may be explosive toward a parent, sibling, spouse, or child. If this is occurring, it is because even though we have matured physically into adults, our emotional being has remained stagnant. We do not grow emotionally when we have been hurt emotionally.

Unfortunately, many of us do not know how to recover from our emotional pain. Instead of addressing the hurt, we simply carry the pain around with us. Even though we may not readily recognize our pain, we realize its presence through the interactions we have with others who accidentally or intentionally "hit our sore spot." For most of us, there is typically at least one family member who knows exactly how to stir up that pain within us. Most of the time they hit our spot intentionally, as if it is part of their goal to see us become dismantled.

Inside of us, most of us know one person who knows how to get to us. When we interact with this person, we are almost waiting for the comments that offend us to begin. We expect conflict of some sort with this person. In most cases, we learn to deal with the conflict by either not saying anything or trying to have quick comebacks that hurt the other. In these cases, we are reacting to the pain that we feel rather than addressing it.

A part of being emotionally mature is being capable of addressing all of our feelings. As an adult, we are now in a position in which we do not have to accept other peoples' treatment of us if it impacts us negatively. Nevertheless, we often continue to allow people to hurt us because we have not known how to take responsibility for our emotions. We react because that is how we have been taught.

Most people have not learned a model for how to honor and accept all of their feelings. What is most often seen are people who either try to push away their feelings or who are completely out of control with their emotions. Neither of those options feels ideal, yet we do not know any other way. We do not know any other way because for so many of us, our emotional growth has ceased. Even though we have continued to grow physically into adults, our emotional reactions may be more like how children attempt to handle their feelings. We must be willing to become conscious in order to address how handling our feelings in a childish manner does not serve our highest good.

Being able to see our emotions as a gift is the way to take responsibility for how we feel and to utilize our feelings to best serve us. Usually we only see our "positive" emotions as a gift and try to push the other feelings away. If we do this, however, we miss out on the adjustments that our emotions are guiding us to make in each relationship and in our emotional development. In order to acknowledge those adjustments, we need to slow ourselves down when we are going through an experience that we wish was not occurring.

One example my client recently shared with me was when she went on a brief vacation. She talked to her Mom, who made a comment like, "I hope you do not plan on retiring there." My client took this as an assault. She felt that her mother was critical and non-supportive of the choices my client made. Rather than just remaining quiet, which was my client's typical reaction, she spoke up to her mother. Her response was to "make a dig" back at her mom.

My client felt better because she was no longer keeping quiet when her mother criticized her, which was an improvement. Nevertheless, my client did not feel good, because she was still unwilling to address her emotions. In order for these types of experiences to stop between herself and her mother, which was her goal, she had to be willing to slow herself down during these interactions. By slowing herself down and consciously listening to how she feels when she gets into a sore subject, she will be able to express herself honestly. Through addressing her emotions honestly, my client is able to bring into her and her mother's consciousness what the underlying meaning of their interaction is truly about for them.

The underlying issue is a power struggle. My client desires and has desired all her life for her mother to be supportive and nurturing of her. Because my client still desires this, she creates experiences in which she looks for her mother's approval. When my client does not receive what she desires, she feels disappointed, frustrated, or hurt.

It is important to note that my client believed she was in pain because her mother would not nurture her, yet the pain was really about my client's unwillingness to support and nurture herself. Her Spirit desires these feelings to come from within and not from the external. Her frustration is present because my client *should* feel frustrated. Her Spirit is wondering how many more years is it going to take to understand that she will not be able to get from her mother what she desires. Her Spirit is frustrated that she continues to seek this from outside herself.

Through my client speaking her truth and sharing her feelings, she will be able to give herself the nurturance and support that she desires. For instance, if she says to her mother something like, "When you make comments like that, I feel criticized and unsupported. Please do not make comments like that to me anymore, or I'll have to get off the phone when you do." As she speaks her truth, she is supporting and nurturing herself, as she honors her feelings. She created boundaries with her mother that state that she is unwilling to accept energy that is not for her highest good. Through this process, she is creating what her soul has longed for her to do, which is to nurture and support herself by honoring her feelings, regardless of whether others agree or disagree with what she feels.

Although being able to slow ourselves down to recognize our truth may seem simple, it takes practice. Most of us are used to reacting in a certain way that is an automatic response. As we work toward remembering to slow ourselves down, we will likely have many experiences in which we forget to do so. The difference will be that we are conscious of the experience and how it is impacting us. The more we are aware of the impact on ourselves, the more we will become conscious of slowing ourselves down in future interactions in order to manifest the changes we desire.

The other piece of why this process can be challenging is our fears. Our fears have told us that to confront the situation, we will likely get hurt. In the case of my client, she fears her mother's retaliation of no longer including her in her life. In other words, she fears she will be dismissed from her mother's heart. The truth is that she already feels this way, and neither of them is truly engaged in the other's life. Thus, in trying to hold back her feelings, she is actually creating her fear. Through being willing to confront her fear of sharing her feelings, she will actually begin to mend the distance that has been a part of their relationship for so long. This occurs as they learn to really address one another rather than just interact with each other based on surface events.

Learning to Trust and Honor Our Inner Voice in Our Relationships with Others

Part of the reason we struggle so much with boundaries is that we are questioning our own inner judgment. We have lost our sense of inner knowingness to the degree that we now question whether it is appropriate to feel the way we do, especially when it comes to those we care about. Just stating that out loud seems absurd, yet I know many of my clients, as well as myself, who have questioned, "Do I have the right to feel this way?" Of course, if we are feeling a certain way, then it is for a reason! There is no wrong or right to how we feel – we are just feeling. When we question whether it is right or appropriate to feel the way we do, we are really still searching for approval from outside ourselves.

Many of us try to modify our feelings in order to stay in the good graces of others or simply because we are afraid that sharing our truth would hurt those we care about. By not being authentic with our feelings, we manipulate our emotions in order to meet the needs of others. In doing so, we are basically telling ourselves that our feelings do not matter. Every time we manipulate our emotions, we lose a part of ourselves. Rather than validating our feelings, we are telling our Spirit that we are not willing to listen to what our inner voice is telling us. The more we ignore our inner voice in order to placate others, the more muffled our Spirit becomes. We are in essence teaching our Spirit that we believe others and their feelings are much more important than ourselves. Perhaps that is what we truly believe.

If others are more important than us, then there is no point to having boundaries. Boundaries are about saying this is what I find important for me and my soul to function while being on this planet. It is about respecting ourselves enough to state that we are unwilling to tolerate anything that is not good for our Spirit. Most importantly, it is about claiming our importance, and asserting that who we are matters simply because we are an expression of God.

Our Spirit's Guidance Comes in All Forms but None That Is Harmful

Now you may be thinking, "What if what I want to tell someone how angry I am at them?" Good, then your Spirit is telling you that your boundaries with this person are not what is best for your Spirit. Just because the message that you are hearing is not necessarily a "positive message" does not mean that it is not from your Spirit. The guidance of your anger is not telling you to cause harm to people – your Spirit would not do that. If that is how you feel, ego is taking over your anger. Your anger is present to allow you to listen to what your Spirit really wants to get across. Your Spirit has been upset because something about that relationship is not good for you, and your Spirit is guiding you to listen.

We are afraid to express our anger because we are afraid of our rage. We only become full of rage when we do not allow our anger to be expressed. As stated in Chapter 4, anger is just a form of sadness due to the pain we have been caused. The more we allow ourselves to express why we are angry, irritated, or frustrated, the less of a need there is to become upset. Those feelings are just like any other feeling we have within ourselves and do not have to be expressed wildly or uncontrollably. These feelings only get that way through years and years of trying to smother them by refusing to admit that our pain exists.

If that rage is within us, it needs to be expressed, but there are options as to how we can let these feelings out of us. Our rage can be expressed to the person who has caused us pain, to a trusted friend, or by journaling. If you feel that rage is consuming you, I suggest you get professional support in order to help move you away from living your life in pain.

Regardless of the degree of our anger, its purpose is to make us aware that our boundaries have been violated. We feel anger because our Spirit wants us to learn from the experience in which we did not protect ourselves. When we continue to allow ourselves to be violated by people, our anger is actually toward ourselves for continuing to make choices that allow someone else to disrespect who we are as spiritual beings. Remember that we always have a choice as to whether to allow that person back into our life in the same manner or not. When we make that choice, boundaries are formed and our anger alleviates itself.

Let's think about how we feel when we do not assert ourselves. We feel manipulated, steamrolled, and used. We blame others for *doing this to us*. However, the truth is that we are now adults who have allowed this treatment to occur. No one can do something to us without our input. This is how powerful we are. Yet we give in and give up on ourselves and our feelings all the time in order not to cause inconvenience to another, possibly hurt another's feelings (even though our own feelings are in pain), or create any sort of confrontation.

When I look back at the many times I did this to myself, I remember how upset and angry I was at those who I felt disrespected me. I used to think, "How could they treat me this way?" Once I began to form boundaries, I would question, "How could I allow them to treat me this way?" Now I question, "How could I treat myself this way?"

Recognizing My Own Blocks to Claiming My Voice

Not too long ago, I was at a park with my children. I saw that one of my sons was in danger of falling. Of course, everything happens so quickly in those instances, but this experience demonstrates how ingrained some of our behaviors are. The quickest way to my son was blocked by a father and his child. Instead of asking them to move, I had to go another minute out of my way to reach my son. Fortunately, I still got to him in time.

After the incident, I was shocked by my reaction. I could not believe I was unwilling to ask someone to move for me in order to ensure the safety of my son! Instead, I created a whole new obstacle for myself to get somewhere just so I would not be what I perceived as an inconvenience or bother to another. "What would they think of me if I pushed my way through them?" Mind you that this is not what I was consciously aware of at the time. It is all so automatic and programmed in my thinking that I have learned to find another way around it, versus using my voice.

When we are givers, we learn to ignore our instincts and feelings. We and those we love can pay the price for our unwillingness to honor ourselves. We find ways around our feelings by trying to convince ourselves that our feelings are somehow not legitimate. When I do not ask someone to move who is in my way, I am saying *to myself* that my worth or value is somehow less than another's. My perception at the time was that their need to be there was greater than mine or that they were there first; they essentially laid claim to that space. Of course, none of this is necessarily true, it is just all based on perceptions. The truth is that our perceptions will be false if we continue to place less value on ourselves and our existence compared to others.

We need to intrinsically know we have a right to be here and have the needs that we have. Many of us don't have a clue about our worth, and we certainly question what real value we bring to the world. With those thoughts, we lose any sense of ability or right to create healthy and healthful boundaries. In other words, we literally lose ourselves because we state over and over to ourselves that we do not matter when we refuse to create boundaries. Thus, we become lost souls wandering the Earth.

We tend to be mad, frustrated, and anxious about the fact that many of us are lost, not knowing what our purpose is, why we are here, or what we are supposed to do. We blame God or our parents or lack of education that we do not have passion and purpose in our lives. Who we do not make responsible is ourselves.

We need to see the connection between listening to our inner voice in the day-to-day parts of life in order to hear that voice guiding us toward what our purpose is. If we squash our feelings and do not find ourselves worthy enough to establish boundaries for ourselves, then our inner voice cannot be heard. Our inner voice is our Spirit, which wants us to know our magnificence. Knowing our magnificence is our purpose here.

Manifesting Lasting Change Requires Creating a Shift within Ourselves

If we want to feel at peace with our relationships, only we can correct the imbalance. Typically we try to correct the imbalance by putting the responsibility on the other person.

That is exactly what I did at first with my friend. I told her how I felt and wanted her to change. I then got the typical result in which the change is short-lived. When we want change from another, it needs to be initiated by them, not us. Otherwise, the change will not last.

The only way to make a lasting change is to create it from within ourselves. By taking responsibility for our own energy output, we create the space for others to do the same. Then when people do give their energy, the effect will be lasting, because they are doing so out of their own desires, not anyone else's. Furthermore, if they choose not to give us their energy, we benefit as well. Now we know not to waste our time and energy because they do not value us in the same manner as we value them. Therefore, in order for us to feel our best, we want to only be with people who value us as much as we value them.

We must also learn to decipher which relationships are for our highest good and which are in some way causing us pain. If we feel worn out after spending time with a certain person, then obviously this person is not what is best for us right now in our lives. Having an equal energy exchange between people in relationships creates balance, which prevents us from feeling drained, exhausted, or frustrated.

For myself, I had to distance myself somewhat from my Mom while I was learning to create boundaries. While I was trying to find my voice, her voice was too dominant when I talked to her on the phone every day. While I was working through my emotions, talking to her once or twice a week was what worked best for me. I was not cutting her out of my life, but I was establishing boundaries that were more appropriate in order for me to mature emotionally. As I developed emotional maturity, I was able to reconnect with my Mom, which felt good to us both. We felt good because I was able to establish appropriate boundaries that allowed us to communicate with one another respectfully as adults. Hence, we cannot always judge when we need to create separation, as it may be what brings the relationship closer in the long term.

Other relationships, we may find, need to be let go of all together. If someone in our life brings out in us feelings of inadequacy, we need to move on immediately. We know this is occurring when we walk away from conversations feeling like we did something wrong, yet again, or that we somehow do not measure up. This type of relationship creates so much emotional clutter that we will never be able to receive what is for our highest good. Instead, we are attracting more of what we do not want because we believe in our inadequacy. Recognize that we must buy into a sense of inadequacy in order for us to stay in a relationship that does not make us feel good. In these cases, we need to cut the emotional cord completely.

Sonia Choquette, a psychic and best-selling author, speaks about how each of us has energetic cords to everyone we are involved with in life. This includes mundane relationships and intimate ones. If we do not completely sever these cords with people who are literally draining our energy, we will continue to leak energy. This loss of energy can add up to causing emotional, physical, and spiritual distress if we are not willing to establish boundaries in which we take care of ourselves.

One of the worst ways people do not cut the ties is with their intimate relationships. They do not want to sever completely the ties with a lover who is not right for them, usually out of a fear of being alone. They hang onto that person, while secretly hoping their soul mate will come along. It will not happen. There is too much emotional clutter getting in the way for us to receive our soul mate when we are hanging on to old emotional ties. Continuing to be afraid of being alone ends up making our fear come true. We will end up with the wrong person if we are unwilling to let him or her go. Staying with someone who is not right for us leaves us feeling alone. Therefore, we need to emotionally and energetically free ourselves of the people who are wrong for us in order to receive the right person.

When our boundaries come from a place of love for ourselves, our boundaries will serve us to stay aligned with our Spirit. When our boundaries are created through our fears of being hurt again, we will feel separation and pain. Most of us will begin with forming boundaries by swaying back and forth from creating boundaries out of fear of not having appropriate boundaries when needed. Once we recognize how good it feels not to allow someone to violate our Spirit, we will have a greater willingness to create boundaries that feel right to our soul. Each time we listen, we are honoring our Spirit, which allows our essence to come through more and more. The more we choose to listen to this voice, the more healthy boundaries will be formed, which will keep us feeling good because we are living in alignment with our Source.

Putting this Chapter into Practice:

1) We will not know our magnificence or our purpose if we are unwilling to use our inner voice. We can create shifts by beginning to use our inner voice in the day-to-day experiences of our lives. Speak up when something does not feel right, share your feelings, state that you will not tolerate a behavior that is hurtful or disturbs your inner peace.

2) Examine a relationship in which you've struggled. Are your short-term needs in alignment with what you ultimately desire in the long run? What changes can you make to ensure that you have appropriate boundaries that will serve your long-term desires?

3) Karla McLaren's book *Energetic Boundaries* discusses ways to envision creating boundaries in a loving way to yourself and others. As you begin to address the emotional aspects of creating boundaries, being able to envision boundaries in a healthy manner may feel supportive to you.

Chapter 8
Owning Our Power

All of the work we have done thus far has been about refining our energy in order that we may become more and more aligned with our truth. Through addressing our fears and acknowledging our emotions, our perspective has changed. As our perspective has changed, we have been able to create boundaries and nurture our inner voice. All of this could not be done without an intense focus of our energy. After all, we cannot go about our efforts willy-nilly, or we would not be able to bring about the changes we have desired to make. The more we are able to refine our energy to support us in living the life we desire, the more we are able to own our true power.

As we refine our energy and own our internal power, we are going to find new blocks appear. The closer we become to truly owning our power, the stronger these blocks and fears appear in order for us to work through any limitations we are putting on our life. The ego tries to speak loudly in order for us to buy into beliefs that do not serve us. This is how the ego tries to remain in control. My life coach once told me to visualize the ego as a wolf. The less we feed the wolf, our ego, the hungrier it gets and utilizes any means possible in order for it to get fed. We feed the ego when we buy into lies and fears that prohibit us from fully owning our power.

What I have found is that as much as we desire to own and realize our power, we are also as equally–if not more so–afraid of the power within us. When we first start seeing how we are able to manifest our desires, we are amazed. Yet when we begin to manifest our true desires and it happens with ease, we freeze. It is almost too much for our minds to wrap around the notion that we can have what we desire with no or little effort. Internally we feel confused from our past and what the present can now mean to us. Let us now examine the common misperceptions and blocks that prevent us from honoring the power within us that we are all meant to realize.

Is It Really Lonely at the Top?

We become afraid that owning our power will leave us standing brightly on top of the world, yet we will be doing so alone. If we recall some of the most common fables about wealthy people, they live a lonely, isolated, and unpleasant existence. Think of the Dickens character Scrooge.

Besides fables, we often hear about scandalous examples of people with money who are unscrupulous, as they are willing to utilize any means to get ahead in life. Yet many of us desire prosperity in our lives. We need to address this discrepancy between the abundance we desire and our misperception of what acquiring wealth equates to. In order for us to manifest prosperity, our view of wealth must be congruent with our heart and soul. If we view money as somehow bad for our overall well-being, we are blocked from creating all we desire to have.

Our misperception about wealth occurs by recognizing the difference in those people who have attained power from an egotistical perspective. With their egos running their lives, they are living their life out of fear, relying on the external for validation. Without this external validation, they are nothing. Therefore, they feel desperate to keep what they have or to make more because that is what their whole existence is based on. The result of their fear-based action creates an internally lonely and petty existence.

On the other hand, when we decide to own our truth, we are recognizing our internal power. Manifesting our desires from our truth means we are aligned with our Spirit, which allows us to open our hearts to everyone. Owning our power from our truth will attract rather than isolate us from others.

Nevertheless, as we work our way to living in alignment with our truth, we will make changes that may bring up our fear of being alone. By following our inner guidance, we are likely giving up habits and friends that are not for our highest good. As we create this change, we may feel like there are few people left who understand and support us. Because this sense of isolation is familiar, our fear of loneliness appears again. Many of us can recall when we dared to own and share our truth, only to feel like an outcast for doing so. We have experienced that demonstrating our power has left us feeling more alone rather than when we simply went along with the crowd. Because this occurred for us when we were young and our sense of identity was reliant on others' validation of us, this was devastating. From our experience, we learned not to let our truth out too much (or not at all) because of how it will impact others.

From a spiritual perspective, we know we will always be cared for and therefore have the relationships in our lives that we desire. As we work toward reclaiming our power, we must remind ourselves that we are simply clearing the space in order to bring into our lives the relationships and experiences that are our ideal. The type of relationships our soul desires are those in which we can allow ourselves to shine. In relationships that are good for us, we can own our truth and those around us can do the same. Because we are attracting those people who have an inner sense of security, our friends and loved ones feel joy for one another as we honor our truth and power. Without clearing the space, there would not be room to establish the type of relationships that support us living our best lives.

Even though we may have decided to pull back from relationships that are not best for our highest good, we remain open to everyone. Because we, too, have been challenged to recognize and own our internal power, we have understanding for those who choose not to know their truth at this time. We will be a model for those who are still afraid that it is unsafe to share our truth.

As our hearts remain open, we will naturally attract into our lives those who desire to live, express, and share their magnificence. By maintaining our focus on the abundance that we have within us, as we know our truth and power, we will have the types of relationships that bring the most happiness and joy into our lives. Through recognizing the gifts we have been given in order to own our power, we will no longer have to fear that it is lonely at the top. In fact, more and more people are being called to own their inner power, which means we will have the greatest of company throughout our journey as we choose to live from our truth.

Fear of Our Demise

Even worse than loneliness or isolation is the message of how owning our power can lead to our suffering and death. Leaders such as the Rev. Dr. Martin Luther King, Jr., and Joan of Arc were killed for owning their power and sharing their truth. Even through the teachings of Jesus Christ, we are shown how he was sought out and killed for owning his power. Although Jesus was loved by many, we also recognize that through him speaking his truth, he was crucified. These experiences become a part of our concept of what it would be like if we were to fully stand in our truth and own our power.

For many of us, there is a fear deep down that may not even be conscious to us. This fear is that if we were to speak and act completely from our truth, it would be the end of our life as we know it. Although many of us may be unhappy with certain aspects of our lives, at least we are still alive. Other times, our fear may not be about actual death but rather the end of living our lives as we have been doing. We take comfort in the fact that our life at least feels predictable. When our life is predictable, we feel we can handle it, as we have become used to our circumstances, even if we do not enjoy all of them.

On the other hand, when we are asked to live from our truth, we are often being told to take that next step with a blindfold over our eyes. This is where we get the expression "taking a leap of faith." When we are able to "take the leap," we will feel a trust within ourselves that we are always going to be taken care of by the Universe. After all, most of us have gone through much more than we would have ever thought possible for us to handle. Yet we did it. We survived. Thus, we must be willing to move past our uncertainty about the outcome of our lives by opening ourselves to the experiences that will bring us to manifesting our hearts desires.

Because so many of us have lost faith, we become unwilling to place our trust in the Universe. We are buying into a limiting mentality when a part of us fears that the higher we have risen to own our power, the farther we have to fall. The truth is that we will never know our future outcome. We can only base our life on what we know we can create in the present. We know for certain how we feel good in the present when we are living passionately.

If our focus is on our future detriment due to owning our magnificence, then we will likely create that experience. Again, our thoughts create our reality. Instead of this fear, we can continue to utilize the skills we have learned to continue manifesting the types of experiences we desire. If our focus remains on that which we desire, we will be living our life with joy and continue to manifest our ideal.

Do I Have What It Takes?

Many of us also fear owning our power because we are afraid we are lacking in some manner to be able to handle the responsibility. We may be saying to ourselves, "Do I really have what it takes to be able to stand in my power?" The answer is that we all have what it takes to manifest our dreams–it is just a matter of being willing. We are all qualified, but no one is going to give us the permission to own our power. We must own it for ourselves.

I have seen in myself and friends that as we begin to escalate toward achieving our success, we all of a sudden become frozen. We become uncertain if we are able to manage all that is coming our way, even though this is what we have desired for years. Many of us fear creating our success stories as they become closer because then we question not only whether we are capable but what will happen if we actually do acquire all we desire? If we have been yearning for more all our life, then it feels scary not to be in that position anymore. Therefore, we must ask if we are willing to make ourselves uncomfortable, to wear new shoes so to speak, and actually be the person that we have dreamed of being.

When it comes down to it, many people do not want what is attached to their success. The "downside" of success may be a sense of further responsibility, more growth, and more choices. This is why even though we do not like feeling stuck or unable to make any progress toward our hearts' desires, we unconsciously choose to stay exactly where we are. Let's face it: staying stagnant feels very safe, because we already know that life. Again, it is the unknown that many of us fear. However, not being willing to face that fear leads to a life that is dull, lifeless, and lacking passion.

We fear the unknown because we do not have any guarantees as to what our future experiences will look like. We try to avoid pain by keeping our lives the same. In doing so, we act as if avoiding taking risks equates to not feeling pain. In fact, the opposite is true. We feel more emotional pain when we allow our fears to control us, keep us small, and make our lives feel limited. This is because whatever our life mission is, we are meant to being doing it. Yet we want to believe that not taking risks is better than going for it because we know we would feel completely crushed if our heart's desires did happen for us as we expected. It takes being able to take a risk and trust in the Universe to make those initial steps of change toward achieving our desires.

Owning Our Truth Allows Us to Let Go of Needing Approval

Another block to owning our power is being stuck looking back on an experience in which we feel we utilized our power unwisely. From those past circumstances, we may have found that not everyone was happy with the decisions or actions we took. Others felt that how we handled the situation was unfair or could have been done better. If part of our agenda, either conscious or unconscious, is to make everyone happy, we will not be able to fully own our power.

As we begin utilizing our inner voice, it is important not to delude ourselves into believing we are so powerful that we can control others. We cannot, because they are equally as powerful. People will think what they want, whether we bow to their every command or refuse to do anything their way. If we are people pleasers, some people will find us nice while others will find us too needy. If we go about life in our own way, some people will find us strong and admirable while others will see us as controlling and selfish. We can no longer trick ourselves into thinking that we can alter ourselves in order to gain approval without consequences to our Spirit. The only control we have is whether or not we will listen to our inner voice.

Once we are willing to accept and honor the truth of who we are, we will not care how others view us because we are no longer vying for their approval. The truth is that once we feel approval, and therefore respect ourselves, others will respect us as well. Even if they do not agree with what our truth is, there will be a sense of respect, because that is the energy that we give to others when we own our truth. Hence, we are less apt to get caught up in others' perceptions because our focus is on having our perceptions aligned with our truth. Having this focus simplifies life. In letting go of our need for approval, we become free. As we live more freely in our truth, we find that everything falls into place in life so much more easily.

As we live from our truth, other people will also be able to recognize how we live life with much more ease. It seems effortless for us to create win-win circumstances with the people who are a part of our lives. People who are like-minded will be drawn to creating the same in their lives as well. Having this magnetism makes creating the reality that we desire happen much more quickly because we become a part of a flow that is tied with the Universe.

Even when our truth does not feel good to others involved, we are still creating the opportunity to correct any imbalances. For instance, when we speak our truth about people slacking off, we are letting them know two things. First, we are demonstrating that we notice that they are not taking responsibility for their part in the relationship, whether work or personal. Second, we are sharing with them that their actions impact us. In doing so, we will feel good for speaking our truth, for not taking responsibility for other peoples' actions, and for allowing people the opportunity to take care of their own responsibilities. Even though in the short term this may not feel good for another person to hear, there will be long-term benefits. Depending on how we shared our truth, we may also come to the realization as to whether the manner in which we discussed our feelings was the best, given the circumstances. Whether it is our own perspective that needs adjusting, the other person's, or both, in the future change can be manifested toward creating greater alignment with our heart's desires.

Remembering the Difference between Owning Our Power through Our Spirit Versus Our Ego

Owning our power spiritually is much different than trying to acquire power from an egotistical prospective. Yet many clients have expressed concern about owning their power because they fear their ego will take over. We fear we will abuse our power because most of us have at one time or another. We must remember that when we misused our power, it was because we were not aligned with our truth and acting out of our fears. It is our ego that convinces us to allow our rational minds to take over our lives in order that our inner voice remains silenced. The ego will only take over when we continue to look outside ourselves for approval.

Success is a form of receiving approval. When we are successful, we are more approved of by society, and typically we feel a greater sense of approval for ourselves. Our successes feel like a form of recognition for our efforts, and sometimes we want that to be validated.

On the other hand, when our sense of success comes from our Spirit, we feel fulfilled, because we are doing what our soul has longed for us to do. We feel satisfaction, joy, and gratitude for being able to express ourselves in this way. Our Source desires and is supporting us to feel this type of success because this is us owning our power.

When we have the feeling that our successes are not enough and we need to strive for more, it is our ego driving us. We are depicting our sense of worth not based on what we are doing or how it makes us feel. Rather, we are creating our sense of worth based on what we have achieved. With our ego guiding us, we will achieve success, feel good, and then suddenly feel empty or let down. We will continue to strive for more and more in order to curb that sense of emptiness. We feel empty because the validation is coming from outside ourselves.

When we strive outside ourselves for approval, we will always feel a sense of lack. Looking for this validation external to us will leave us with a sense that there is never enough. When our focus is external, we feel the need for more and more things, whether money, shoes, homes, boats, clothes, etc. When we are feeling lack, it is true, but not in the sense that we are lacking anything that we actually need. The sense of lack we are truly feeling is for love, honor, and respect for ourselves.

Instead of projecting our sense of lack onto the external, we need to be addressing this from within ourselves. If we choose not to address this, we will continue to feel that what we have is somehow not enough and want more as a means to validate that we are enough. For this reason, many people acquire the sense of status or success that they have always dreamed about and then do not feel good. Often they feel let down, because achieving this success was supposed to make them feel happy and at peace. Outside success never will. However, because most people are not willing to accept this, they continue to want more. Thus, if we derive our sense of self based on external concepts, our happiness and sense of peace will always be fleeting.

Creating Internal Validation

How, then, do we acquire being able to validate ourselves? After we have addressed our fears and admitted our feelings, we reach a point at which we need to confront head on any lingering messages we are holding on to that do not serve us. As always, we must check in with ourselves. Are the messages we are hearing our truth? If not, then they are the lies that our ego is using to keep us safe. If we can provide ourselves with proof that the lies are not our truth, we will begin inhibiting those messages. By providing proof of our truth, we are reinforcing ourselves to turn to our internal knowingness rather than our default reaction of fear. Because our fear is based on wanting external approval, we are teaching ourselves to check in with our internal truth and power. The concrete evidence against our fears gives our mind an alternative belief to wrap around rather than the lies our ego has us believe in order to stay safe. Write to ourselves, say our truth out loud, and acknowledge our truth rather than the lies. Having the proof of how our truth has served us written out in black and white allows us to override the messages of our ego.

Being aware of our internal process, we are able to recognize when we are beginning to stray away from being aligned with our Spirit before we swing too far on the continuum from our desired state. If we do not catch this imbalance quickly enough and refuel our Spirit, we will experience pain in order to help us return our focus internally. The more accustomed we become to doing this for ourselves, the less dramatic swings in our feelings we will have. We will recognize that when we begin to feel down, we are beginning to buy into the lies once again.

By being attuned to our feelings, we can quickly address our imbalance. The quicker we address our imbalance by nurturing and honoring our truth, the less pain and suffering we will feel. We regain our sense of inner balance and peace when we allow ourselves to let our truth come through regardless of the reactions of others. It is that simple, yet we all need to come back to the inner knowingness that our truth will indeed set us free. As with anything, the more practice we have in simply being who we are, regardless of others' reactions, the more at ease we will feel internally.

When we are in the midst of some sort of inner turmoil, it is important to remember that the answers are always within us. Nevertheless, we need to be willing to ride out the wave of turmoil. Even if we do not know yet what the answers are, we are being guided to them. When the answers emerge quickly, we are able to move past our discord with ease. What is more challenging is to find peace even when we do not have the answers yet. At these times, it is crucial to take time to reconnect with what organically brings us happiness and fuels our souls. Furthermore, this is our time to focus even more intently on that which we desire. This is our time to tap into our faith.

From the beginning of our work, it has taken courage to acknowledge how we have been living, address what we have bought into that is not true, and be willing to listen to our truth. Oftentimes we did not want to do this work because we knew intuitively that it would create an upheaval in our lives. Now we are being asked not only to have courage but unwavering faith that we truly have the power within us to create the life we desire. If our faith wavers, we can ask for assistance toward keeping us in the Universal truth that our needs will be addressed. Once we are able to place our trust in ourselves and in the Universe, we are able to recognize the freedom in owning our truth.

As we become used to living from our truth, we will find issues that once would have caused a sense of upheaval in our lives are now merely small waves we need to ride. When we can recognize this change within us, we know we are living in alignment with our truth and Spirit. This alignment brings us peace, as we know our worth, our beauty, and our magnificence from within rather than from anyone or anything outside of ourselves. This is what is meant by living. Living freely is the true meaning of owning our power.

Being able to validate for ourselves the changes we have made and our own efforts to achieve them is imperative for being able to own our power. Without being able to do this for ourselves, we cannot be free. We will remain trapped trying to seek the approval of others, which in effect takes us away from our true path. If we can approve of ourselves, then we can listen to our inner guidance telling us what the next step is. Trusting in your inner guidance will allow you to actually take that next step, even if appears as if your life is not working out as you desired. Having this belief in yourself and in the Universe means you feel aligned to your Spirit. Feeling aligned with your Spirit brings peace.

My Process of Owning My Truth and Authentic Power

My desires have scared me at times. They are so powerful that I make them into reality in my head. My fear asks me to ponder, "What if they never happen?" The bottom line is that

I know I'll be led through my experiences to attain all that my soul desires. I have no guarantee that how I would picture my life to turn out will actually occur. All I know is that I need to put my energy in the direction that my Spirit is guiding me in order for my dreams to have the chance to exist.

Maybe my dreams will come true and maybe they will not. My ego strives for me to know my worth through receiving approval by attaining success. My Spirit's desire, however, is to know my part in the Divine's plan by fully expressing my Spirit and enjoying the abundance of the Universe. Because I know God has always provided me with my heart's desires, I know that those aspects that are a part of my heart will be cared for and nurtured. Although my dream could or could not happen as I intend it, quite frankly it does not matter. It does not matter because I know through experience that if what I desire does not happen in the time frame that I thought it would or exactly how I envisioned it, this is only because I am going to be receiving beyond my dreams. I know this because I know I am *always* cared for by the Universe, *always*.

My fears often occur because I do not see the next steps, and I am not being given a guarantee that my heart's desire will come true. It is a truth that nothing is a guarantee. Therefore, it is my job to be open to the gifts that accompany not having a guarantee. This includes being willing to accept the gifts that come in packages that I am not expecting.

Being able to accept unexpected gifts reminds me of getting pregnant for the first time. I was not trying to get pregnant, as I was in the middle of completing my doctoral program. Nevertheless, I was immediately excited when I found out I was pregnant. My fears were also present as I became concerned about how I would complete my program, which was my dream at the time. After all the hard work I had done, it was a big priority to me to earn my doctorate. Furthermore, my ego loved the idea of being called "Dr. Bersell."

Throughout my pregnancy and a short while after my daughter was born, I was determined to still complete my doctorate. After all, I had finished all the coursework. All that I had left to complete was an internship and dissertation. The dissertation did not scare me. What I did not want, however, was a full-time internship while raising my daughter. My heart knew that I would not feel good being apart from my newborn baby. If I chose to complete my doctorate, I recognized that the time away from my daughter would not end with the internship. After completing an internship, I would have had to work full time in order to qualify for licensure. I realized that if I chose to continue and complete my internship and licensure hours, I would be much more separated from my baby than I would ever desired to be. My heart's desire of feeling connected to my newborn outweighed my ego's desire to be called Dr. Bersell.

I made the decision to finish my degree with a master's, even though I had spent an extra year in coursework and training for my doctorate. My friends thought I was crazy letting go of my doctorate. They thought it was such a waste of my time and money not to have my doctorate to demonstrate all the work I had done.

Once I had recognized my truth, the decision was not a difficult one, because I knew within my heart that I had made the right decision for me. It had been challenging for my ego that I was not going to receive that external validation of achieving my doctorate degree. Nevertheless, my heart knew that in closing this door, I was actually opening another, which it was my destiny to follow.

In leaving the doctoral program, I completely trusted my heart. Although others thought I was crazy for leaving all my hard work behind, I did not look back on my decision with regret. There was nothing to regret, because I knew at the time within my soul that my course was about to change toward what I was truly meant to do in life. My experience would have been much different if my soul's expression meant becoming a licensed clinical psychologist. I knew at that time, however, that a traditional psychology role was not a part of my path. Having this inner sense of knowingness allowed me to take the leap of faith to let go of what I initially thought was my path to success. Everything that I had gone through in my program, I recognized, was preparation. Through the program, I gained the confidence and experiences I would need in order to be able to create my true heart's desire, even if I no longer knew exactly what that was.

As I look back, the preparation I received has been perfect for my journey. Prior to my psychology program, I would have never thought myself smart enough to achieve a doctorate. Even though I did not complete my degree, being top in my class gave me the confidence in myself that I was intelligent. Furthermore, my program allowed me to learn and become comfortable with writing, which was something I was phobic about prior to beginning the program. Because ninety percent of my program's evaluation was based on what I wrote, I had no choice but to work through my fears about writing. Lastly, the program gave me the opportunity to recognize my own need for addressing my pain. In doing so, I met incredibly wise people.

One of the greatest gifts I received was the realization that all aspects of our pain are not attended to in traditional psychotherapy. This realization led me to look outside of traditional psychotherapeutic treatment modalities in order to address my own blocks. Even though I had addressed the pain that was inhibiting me from living a full life, I still had blocks that prevented me from experiencing life's fullness. My process led me to my passion of living life in complete connection to my truth.

For all of those experiences that led me to living in my truth, I am grateful. Although my expectation of finishing my doctorate did not happen, I was able to recognize the gift. Fortunately, I could see that with ease at the time, so there was little pain involved. The pain that occurred only lasted when I was trying to hang onto an old dream that did not suit me any longer. Once I let go and opened myself up to new possibilities, the pain and fear were gone.

My heart has allowed me to recognize that I got from the program what I needed. My heart also realizes that I do not need a doctorate for the work that I am intended to do. Surprisingly, other people continue to struggle with me not completing my degree with greater difficulty than I have had in letting go. I am often asked if I'll ever go back and finish my degree, because their mind cannot comprehend my not receiving the validation for the work I had done. What I cannot explain is that I feel very strongly that I am on the path I am intended to live. What is often missed is the fact that my education is not lost. It is a part of me, whether that is recognized through a degree or not.

What I have realized is that when people feel what I am doing is crazy, it usually means I am making a good decision for myself. Making decisions that are not ordinary or that involve risk is par for the course of living a unique and amazing life. Otherwise our fears can paralyze us if we allow them to shape our lives. This occurs because our ego is trying to convince us to lead our lives based on our heads instead of our hearts. My ego tries to convince me to listen to "my voice of reason." This voice is the one that tells me to think things through, be logical, and have a plan. My heart, on the other hand, tells me to listen to my gut. This voice I like a lot, because it is the one that leads me on adventures, fills my life with passion, and keeps me energized and guessing about life.

If I listen to the voice of reason, it only sheds light on all my fears. It tells me, for instance, that to create and have the career I desire is impossible, because I would never have the time to dedicate to it, that there would be too much work, and that I would end up feeling stressed. My gut, however, tells me to take a chance. It is my gut that tells me that going for my career will fuel me, rather than deplete my energy and passion for life. My gut also tells me that although going for my dream career will be challenging at times, it will teach me the lessons I need to learn in order to grow further as a person.

Our ego's job is to keep us safe and out of any potential circumstances in which our true gift–our Spirit–could be hurt. In doing so, however, we lose the opportunity to share our gift with the world, which is our purpose. Our heart's job is to remind us to listen to our inner voice, which is always there guiding us. Therefore, as much as my ego wants me to buy into that what I fear is not having my dreams fulfilled, I recognize the truth: *My ego's fear is that I will have my dreams fulfilled.*

If my dreams were fulfilled, there would be no need for my ego. My ego is fighting for its life when it limits me by trying to fuel my fears. The more I challenge these fears and listen to my inner voice, the more proof I have that my inner guidance is always what is best for me. In fact, I have learned that by following my gut, life actually feels easier, more purposeful, and richer. This is why when it comes to many decisions, I turn off that voice of reason because there are many more rewards in following my gut instead.

I am grateful that my doctoral program door closed for me in order that another door–involving coaching, writing, and speaking–has opened for me. If we look back on our lives through our hearts and not our egos, we will see how failed experiences are really gifts of new opportunity to become more aligned with our truth and purpose. This is not just my story but everyone's story, if we are willing to listen and trust.

Trust that we are loved more than our conception of what love is. When we do, we will see that our Creator is not only taking care of our needs but is taking care of our soul in ways that we may not ever fully comprehend. Remember, though, that our life will only go this way if we choose to believe in the Divine's amazing love for us at all times. We are never forgotten about, never abandoned, and never alone. We are all surrounded by the Universe's love always and will see more evidence of this if we choose to believe this is so. Therefore, we need to choose to see this in our lives by being grateful for how well our Source has taken care of us even amidst all our doubts. We are still here, we have survived everything, and we are reading these words that are here to urge us to listen. Listen and know your truth. We are being guided right now, yet only if we allow ourselves to be.

Putting this Chapter into Practice:

1) Recall an experience in which you succeeded in owning your power. Recognize the impact that carries on within you. Now do the same with an experience in which you felt ashamed for not being able to own your power. Journal about how that has affected your sense of self. Search for the truth of the matter.

2) Write your life's dream story. Utilize all the experiences that you have had, especially those that have challenged your expectations as to how they have supported you to manifest your ideal life.

3) Envision what challenges you may foresee as you claim your dream. Be willing to ask for support with those fears, whether that is through opening up your limited perception or through providing the help you need to feel more at peace with manifesting your dream.

Chapter 9
Abundance

Many people feel challenged when it comes to manifesting their desires. We may put out to the Universe exactly what we want, yet we do not truly believe that our dream will ever happen. Some of us may believe in our dream; however, when the dream does not happen, we get angry, frustrated, and disappointed. These experiences occur because there is more to receiving than most people realize.

The Universe gives us exactly what we are open and capable of receiving. This is the Law of Attraction. We cannot fool the Universe if we are "trying to stay positive" and believe in our dream when there is a larger part of us that does not believe in ourselves. In this chapter, we will address the most common blocks that inhibit us from opening ourselves to the Universal flow of abundance that is there for us all.

Learning to Open the Door to Receive

Before we are able to attain what we desire, we must first be receptive to the possibility of receiving. Part of making ourselves open and receptive is clearing the way. Picture that there is a door of abundance within each of us. Is yours cluttered with people, objects, and habits that are not for your highest good? If this is the case, the door has no way of even being cracked open let alone be open wide enough for all the abundance that you desire.

In order for us to be open to receiving the abundance of the Universe, we need to make sure we are doing our part to clear the path. Otherwise, if we are so bogged down with what is not for our highest good, we will only push aside the gifts that are being given to us. The gifts we desire the most will end up tossed aside. Even if the gift somehow makes its way through to us, we may not be able to recognize it as a gift because we are so overwhelmed by our clutter. Rather than being able to see the gift as a blessing, it feels like another burden or an added responsibility.

Continue to Clear away the Clutter in Our Lives

Throughout this book, we have been addressing how to clear out our clutter. When I speak about clutter, I mean physical, emotional, and spiritual clutter, all of which take us away from connecting with and living from our truth. The closer we move toward creating the life we desire, the more we will be asked to fine tune our life. As we are now addressing how to manifest the abundance that we desire, there is more for us to be aware of that can inhibit our ability to take into our lives all that we desire. Let us look at the common inhibitors to creating abundance in our lives.

Physical Clutter

When I speak about physical clutter, I mean all the objects that are a part of our daily life. We need to get rid of what we are not using in order to free ourselves up to receive what we truly desire. If we are complaining that there is not enough room, then there really is not room for more of the physical abundance we want to manifest. Recycle, donate, and clear it out. This is pertinent, especially if we are feeling disorganized or buried under piles of paperwork.

Developing an organizational strategy will help maintain being able to put our energy toward our desires rather than toward objects that no longer serve us. Once we do, we will feel refreshed, because we have gotten rid of stagnant energy that was weighing us down. Clearing the physical objects that no longer serve us is one way to clear the path to receiving again.

Another aspect to what clutters us physically is the food we put into our bodies. Are you cluttering your physical body with poor nutrients, chemicals, and trans fats? Do you even know what exactly is going in your body when you eat? If our bodies feel weighed down by the food we are eating, there is less room for our energy to flow toward creating abundance.

For the longest time, I did not realize how significant nutrition is to creating my ideal life. I was fortunate that I could eat anything without becoming overweight. Then I started to have one health issue after another. The first was my ulcer and then came the reappearance of cervical dysplasia. My intuition kept telling me this was about how I fuel myself. I was taking great care of my spiritual and emotional needs, yet without this physical component, I was imbalanced. I had to clear the food clutter and honor how I fueled my body. I went from being semi-conscious of what I eat to incorporating the natural abundance that the Earth gives us into all my meals. Vegetables have become the foundation of my meals when before they were almost nonexistent. Furthermore, I choose organic foods while also limiting my sugar and alcohol intake. Now when I eat the rich greens of the Earth, I feel as if I am taking in abundance, which properly fuels me to have the energy I need to create my ideal life. In my mind, I eat abundance to create abundance.

Emotional Clutter

Our emotional clutter is comprised of relationships and habits that no longer serve us. If life does not feel the way we desire, it is because we have created it that way. We now know to let go of the fear and pain and the relationships that are not for our highest good; doing that work has freed us. Still, we must continue to examine if there are elements to our life that need changing or if there are those that we have felt challenged to let go of in order to live our best life.

I feel that I must frequently reexamine my life to determine what is working for me and what is not. Our reality is that we are constantly changing. In order to stay on top of being able to manifest our desires, we must remain conscious about how we are living our life. Each day we redefine exactly what we want by our actions, thoughts, and feelings. By staying conscious of our emotional state, we are able to determine what we need to change and what can stay the same. Our efforts to stay conscious support us to have a clearer vision of what we truly desire.

In my life, I need to redefine not only what works for me but for my family as well. The emotional environment I create in my home has a significant impact on all of my family members. Because my children's needs are constantly changing, I cannot hold onto habits, behaviors, or actions that are no longer serving us even if they worked wonders a month ago. Although this takes some energy and attention, it is always worth it to me. Being willing to address our changing needs allows me to continue to create balance and peace in our lives, which allows me to feel free.

Even though we have done so much to work through our emotional blocks, we cannot stop utilizing our emotions as a tool to continue to refine our energy to its highest potential. We must remember that repeated feelings and experiences keep reappearing in order to get our attention. Our Spirit is guiding us to utilize our energy to create necessary change so we will no longer have this "energy leak." Trusting our inner wisdom to lovingly guide us will support us to feel more emotionally at peace, which creates the space for the abundance of inspiration and creativity to come through to us.

Spiritual Clutter

Our spiritual selves are deeply tied to our emotional well-being, so getting rid of our emotional clutter will do wonders for our Spirit. We can also address spiritual clutter by seeing what stands in the way of creating intimacy and connection with our Creator and our true selves. Examine old beliefs that are not aligned with the truth of us all being a part of our loving and caring Source. For example, ask yourself if you fear God in any way, if you believe it is possible to have an intimate connection with the Divine, or if you have trust and faith in a Higher Being's presence in your life. Our answers to these questions can reveal notions that keep us disconnected from our spirituality, which fuels our well-being.

If we have spiritual clutter, we need to ask our inner voice for guidance toward how we can receive support for removing these blocks. Trust and listen for our voice to work through us, such as when we are drawn to go to a certain event or a friend recommends a book along the same topic that addresses this issue. There is support out there, yet we may have to allow ourselves to expand beyond our comfort zone in order to gain the spiritual insight that allows us to feel at peace again with our Source. By having faith that our inner voice will always guide us, we will be led toward what we are longing for in our hearts.

One of my biggest spiritual blocks was my unconscious anger at God. After working through my emotional blocks of hurt, rage, and sadness toward people in my past, I still felt inhibited about experiencing joy. After wrestling for months with what was still causing me sadness, I realized that my inability to experience joy was due to my anger toward the Divine. Little did I realize I was angry for having to go through this human experience and all the pain that I felt was associated with living. I felt tricked into coming here on this physical plane, and I no longer wanted to deal with the struggle.

In order for me to feel comfortable addressing my feelings toward my Creator, I first had to change my thoughts about God. Many of the teachings that I had learned about God growing up did not make sense to me in my heart. In my heart, I felt love was the embodiment of our Source, yet I was taught to believe that God was someone or something I should fear. Even though I felt love from God, I still bought into believing that God was punishing, vengeful, and, if provoked, full of rage. As an adult, I had to reconnect with what my heart told my about my Creator rather than what religion told me I ought to believe. Through my honest evaluation of my spiritual beliefs, I was able to align the guidance I received from my heart with the spiritual aspects of my upbringing that felt true to me.

My inner voice guided me beyond the original parameters that compromised my notions of God. As my notions of God felt more aligned with what my heart had told me was true, I felt more connected to the Divine than I ever had before. Even though in my past I was very devout, the fear I felt created a chasm in my relationship with my Creator. I came to a point, however, when I could no longer hide behind a sense of gratitude and love for my life. In a moment, all of the frustration and anger I felt toward my Source came pouring out of me. What was interesting was that allowing myself to share my true feelings actually made my relationship more intimate with God rather than feeling damned as I previously feared. In my youth, I would have felt guilty or worried that I would somehow be punished for being angry toward God. The truth was that in being vulnerable with my Creator, I was able to deepen my relationship. Deepening my spiritual relationship supported me to find the spiritual peace, guidance, and understanding that I have desired for so long.

What I learned from that experience is that if there are aspects of our lives (or our lives in general) that need clarification from God, we need to ask for the Universe's support to receive understanding. If we do not feel at peace with our existence here, we must go to our Source. Allowing ourselves the intimacy to express our truth, whatever it may be, is crucial to our spiritual growth.

We may feel frustration when we do not understand or cannot hear direct communication from our Source. In addition, we may feel anger for the lack of direction or purpose in our lives. Sadness may also permeate our lives just because we are here and our life feels too much like a challenge. Whatever our feelings, the Universe desires us to express them so that we can move past the anger and create more intimacy in our lives.

If we are still mad at our Creator, we will not be able to openly receive all that our Source desires for us to receive. We are not completely open to receive when we are unable to understand all the gifts we have already been given. As we come to find peace with the Divine, we will be freeing ourselves from the biggest unconscious inhibitor. Only then are we truly open to experience the magnificence, joy, and abundance that our Creator desires for us to have in life.

As we address the physical, emotional, and spiritual aspects of our lives, we can visualize the clutter surrounding our door of abundance begin to clear. The more we are able to clear away the clutter, the easier the door will be to open. As we learn to open the door of abundance, we must work toward keeping that door wide open. In order to do this, we must stay on top of what we are accumulating energetically by determining if it is still serving our highest good.

We determine what is for our highest good based on how we feel. If we are feeling drained, we need to look for the source and ask ourselves, is it a physical, emotional, or spiritual drain we are feeling? Trusting our gut to guide us will support us to know what is right for us to let go of at this time. When we do, we will recognize the amazing abundance that is there supporting, guiding, and providing for us.

After Clearing Our Clutter, We Must Focus Our Energy on Our Desires

Once we have cleared the space of our clutter, we must also be willing to do our part in making our dreams a reality. It is a blessing to believe in our dreams and trust they will occur, because we know we are always supported by the Universe. Nevertheless, we cannot rely on the Universe to simply hand our dreams over to us. We have to really know within our hearts that we are willing to put our energy toward creating our dream life.

Putting our energy toward our dream does not mean that we are meant to run ourselves ragged. Excessive doing is based on fear and lack, not abundance. Our energy needs to begin with being focused on the inner experiences that we desire to have more often in our life. Thus, our energy should focus on being rather than doing. When we allow ourselves to be authentically in our truth, we are connecting to our inner Source, which has a constant flow of abundance running through us. It is our job to know how to be conscious of the abundance within ourselves.

Based on Western standards, we have misunderstood how to truly create a dream life. Typically people put all their energy toward their careers in order to attain their dream; in the process, they neglect their inner essence. The result is people feeling unfulfilled in some aspect of their life. Therefore, even if we create the external vision of our dream, it will be meaningless if we do not feel whole internally.

By building a foundation within ourselves, we can truly recognize and enjoy all the abundance the Divine desires us to experience. Our energy is best utilized in learning how to create the joy, peace, and love for life that we all desire. As we learn how to do this for ourselves, we become in touch with what brings us joy, which draws us closer to understanding our purpose and passion. Even when we do not know exactly what our passion is, if we are attuned to our truth, we will know what our Spirit is guiding us to do next. In order to make our dream our reality, we need to follow that guidance, which creates many opportunities for the Universe to jump in and assist us when the time is right.

By committing our action toward what it is that we desire to experience in life, we are demonstrating our dedication toward fulfilling our purpose. In dedicating ourselves, we are indicating that we are ready to put the energy toward creating abundance first and foremost within ourselves. This discipline of creating abundance within ourselves will support us when we are guided toward our life's purpose. Ultimately our internal work brings us to knowing our inner strength and power, which is then utilized toward taking the necessary risks to achieve our ideal life. Because our passion is fueling us, we feel that there is no other option for us but to continue on this path. Furthermore, we will have all the energy we need to put toward creating our ideal. Of course, it will take effort on our part to make our ideal occur. This effort is twofold. One aspect of the effort we need is assertive movement toward making our dream a reality. The second aspect is our need to continue to check in with ourselves internally to remain connected to our inner Source, which guides us to the abundance we desire to create. Our energy source is being fueled by the desire to fulfill our purpose rather than trying to determine how our choices will serve us toward achieving some standard of success. When we are motivated internally, anything is possible!

Regardless of whether our hearts' desires are about finding a mate, creating a dream career, or losing weight, we must be willing to put our energy toward that goal. As I mentioned in Chapter 2, energy can mean investing the time or money to get the support that will help us make it happen. Many times people look at getting assistance as expensive, whether it is a coach, therapist, trainer, or nutritionist. What price can we put on making the necessary shifts in order for our dream life to occur? When we have tried it on our own and our life still is not how we desire it to be, we need to put the energy toward our dream in order to make it happen. We need to demonstrate that our internal needs are worth our time and energy. Once we take care of our inner needs, our outer world will reflect the peace, joy, and abundance that is within us.

People would probably fall over if I added up all the money and time I have put toward my personal growth. Even though there was no immediate payback in financial terms, I intuitively knew when it was time for me to address these aspects of my life. Sometimes the aspects of my life appeared to have nothing to do with the future accomplishments I desired to experience. Yet I needed to address every aspect of my life in order to build a solid foundation from which my desires could continue to build. I also recognized that the energy I put toward any of my passions would come back to me tenfold. The truth is that there is no dollar amount I can put on changing my past living conditions, which were filled with anxiety and insecurity, into living a joyful, purposeful, and passionate life. When we take a step back, we all can recognize that investing in ourselves and our Spirit is priceless.

Healing Our Concept of Abundance

The main block that inhibits people from taking action is their concept of abundance. There are people on both ends of the spending continuum when it comes to their sense of abundance and prosperity. There are those who are extremely budget oriented, while there are others who spend excessively. Neither of these extremes is good for our soul. If we spend excessively, our soul is weighed down constantly because we are trying to fulfill ourselves through the external. When we are extremely tight with our spending, our soul feels so squeezed that there is no room for our Spirit to breathe, let alone shine. Neither of these extreme cases demonstrates an accurate perception or a trust in the abundance of the Universe.

When people spend excessively, they are spending more than they have because a part of them believes the Universe will never truly provide for their desires. Internally there is little or no sense of abundance for people who spend excessively. Because deep down they feel a sense of emptiness, excessive spenders never reach a saturation point. They will always want more due to their sense of lack from within. In a sense, they are hoarding because they bought into a concept that there will not be enough to get around to them and they must take for themselves.

This mentality of hoarding can be innate, which I'm reminded of by my twin sons. If we look at money as energy, my twin sons fight over their main energy in their life, which is food. When food is given to them, they are both scrambling to get their share. They have this mindset that there may not be enough for both. They shove food into their mouths and eat as quickly as possible so they can ask for more. Trust me, I am not starving my kids! I feel this may have been their experience in the womb, where they felt they had to fight each other to survive. Now they try to hoard every bit of food at the beginning of each snack or meal just so they know their needs will be satisfied.

Given this example, it may be important to ask yourself if there is something about your family dynamic that plays into feeling that there may not be enough to go around for everyone. It may also have been a seemingly small experience, such as being at a party and all the kids got a balloon but you. Don't discount either of these types of scenarios toward how they may be impacting your sense of abundance. It is also important to note that even given the same or similar experience, people may react differently. Although some may feel that they must accumulate beyond their actual needs due to their fear of lack, others will stockpile what they have for the very same reason.

Those who limit their spending quite severely also have a mindset of lack of abundance. They, too, fear that their needs will not be taken care of by the Universe. Living from a sense of lack attracts more lack in their lives, which reiterates their fear that there will not be enough for them. They convince themselves that they cannot afford anything that they truly desire. Inside they feel depleted because they are not providing enough to fuel their soul.

Abundance is a perception, and money is only energy. If we excessively utilize our energy in areas that are not for our highest good, then we will not have the necessary energy we need to provide for our basic needs. If we keep the energy we have all bottled up, then our energy has no outlet to support us living a full, happy, and passionate life. Balance is acquired by putting in enough energy toward all aspects of ourselves, which include the crucial elements of our basic physical, emotional, and spiritual needs.

Unfortunately, many people lose an accurate perception of abundance, buying into the notion that they are doing all they can just to survive. I understand this and have been there, yet I know this is not the truth. The truth is we attract into our lives what we believe. If we believe that times are tough, then they will continue to be tough. However, if we switch our perception to remembering that all our needs will always be provided for, then we will attract more of what we want being provided to us.

Even if our life does not yet look like the dream we envisioned, we have manifested our current existence. We will open ourselves to receive more when we are able to recognize the abundance we have created in the present. When we see that all our creations have occurred in order for us to live the life we desire, we will realize that we are on our way to manifesting all our hearts' desires.

Finding Balance in My Perceptions of Abundance in My Life

Not too long ago, I went through a period in which I felt like my family was barely skimming by to keep what possessions we had. Money was tight after dealing with a housing project in which we were swindled out of tens of thousands of dollars. This happened to occur at the same point I gave birth to my seven-week-premature twin sons. Because of some insurance glitch that occurred when we moved from Illinois to Wisconsin, our boys' hospital bills were not covered. The bill for their hospital stay was over $100,000 per boy! Their five-and-a-half weeks in the hospital would bankrupt us if we had to pay for their stay on our own. We were brought to our knees in fear of losing everything we had.

We were fortunate to find emergency insurance and support. Although the insurance did not cover the costs completely, our bills were significantly reduced. Nevertheless, between the hospital bills we did owe and our housing project gone very much awry, money was tight. Going to Target felt like an indulgence. During that point in my life, I had many fears about not having my family's needs met. After about a year-and-a-half of living from a place in which I feared that we would never recover from our financial woes, I was brought to face the truth.

Living from a place of lack, I felt limited, tired, and angry. As I began to feel tired of those feelings, I was able to recognize that my sense of lack was all a perception. The truth was that all my needs were still provided for in my life. We were not bankrupt and I did not experience financial ruin. Yes, we had less money, but our needs were being met. I then decided to let go of the notion that we do not have enough abundance.

The truth was that our needs were always met. Knowing this, I let go of my perception of lack and knew that we could afford what we needed as well as that which our soul desired. Instead of feeling we could not afford anything besides the basics, I allowed myself an occasional splurge on an outfit or a pedicure. Each and every time, we had the money to pay for it in addition to still having savings. Having these small indulgences periodically uplifted my soul and allowed me to continue to trust that I will be taken care of as I desire to be. At the same time, I was more adamant about giving myself the time I needed to nourish my soul.

The balance for me was being realistic about our financial circumstances while listening to my soul's needs. Being realistic went from feeling lack to taking responsibility for what I have been given. Whatever abundance I am provided with is present to support me. I now have the option of choosing how I would like this energy to support me. Nothing therefore is "too expensive," it is just a question of determining where I want that energy to go in my life. Perceiving money in this manner allowed me the room to provide for my Spirit as well as for the rest of the needs in my family.

Allowing my Spirit to be nurtured permitted my soul to dance again, as I recognized that the floor was not going to fall out from underneath me. In the long run, taking care of myself brought me to a place of inspiration to jump-start my career again. Knowing that caring for my soul is always a benefit supported me to move from a place of lack to knowing the truth about abundance.

The Gift of Recognizing Abundance in All

Abundance is a sense of knowing what is true and what is real before it even exists. Abundance is the love of the Universe nurturing us and taking care of us through ourselves if we allow ourselves this experience. We all have abundance in some form. It is our job to open our eyes not only to see the abundance we already have but also the potential for abundance in all that is already. Even if we feel lack in a certain area—whether it is love, money, friendships, or our sense of our beauty—we need to see what is already given to us in that area. If we feel there is little or nothing, then thank God that there is so much potential there for this area of life to improve toward how we desire life to actually be. Then see it as changed. See in your mind's eye how you desire your life to be and give thanks for how it is currently filled with the potential to create this change.

For instance, if we desire a loving relationship yet we are alone, we can be grateful for not being in an empty relationship that would block our ability to create that dream. If our career is not going in the direction we thought it should be, we can feel blessed that we are being shown a new way to express ourselves in the world. The list can go on and on. This is not wishful thinking. It is the truth. We simply need to be willing to see the truth for what it is rather than make ourselves the victim of life.

When I am seeing the truth and the abundance that I am surrounded with, I realize that all my desires have come true. They may not have happened in the time frame I desired, but they happened. Life feels magical when I focus on all that I have been given. Am I lucky? No, I am blessed–and we all are.

What I have believed in is the potential for my heart's desires to come true. I believed they could actually happen. All we need to do is look back in our lives and find one example in which something we desired happened and see that the potential is there. Too often we look instead toward all the times that something we desired did not occur. If that is our focus, we will be unable to attract what it is we desire. Instead, we are attracting more unpleasant experiences. If we hold onto the example of when our heart's desire did occur, we realize that there is potential in everything and anything.

The truth is that there is not anything that is hopeless, since through our hopelessness, we find what is real and true to us. As we feel a sense of hopelessness, we are able to weed out what is truly significant to us and why it has meaning to us. If we allow ourselves to feel the hopelessness within us, we will be brought back to our core truth. This truth is that our heart's desires cannot be taken away. They just may not occur in the form that we expect.

Seeing the potential and abundance in all of life does not mean everything that happens to us will occur the way we want it to happen. The wisdom of the Universe is beyond our comprehension. As mentioned in the previous chapter, we will always be given the opportunity to choose to believe in our power and potential–or not. This power is to see our own magnificence and recognize the gift and beauty in all of the life we've been given.

When I look back at some of the things I deeply desired, I am so incredibly grateful they did not occur when I initially wanted them to or not at all. Why? Some things I desired were not meant for me to experience, such as dating Rick Springfield or being on a soap opera. Those experiences were simply not a part of my long-term purpose. Other desires I had hoped for early on, yet came much later. Looking back, I am able to recognize that my desire ended up coming at a perfect time in my life as I share below. The timing was perfect, because if the experience had occurred when I desired it to, I would not have been ready either emotionally or spiritually. I needed to grow as a person in order to handle the extent of the desire I wanted to create. If I were to have had my desire at that time, I would have ended up losing it because I would not have been able to handle it.

An Example of Demonstrating Why Timing Is Crucial to Our Desires

Since my early twenties, I had the desire to get married. However, at that early age, I did not have enough experiences to be ready for the man of my dreams. When I desperately desired to be married, I did not feel about myself what I needed to feel in order to attract the man of my dreams. The man of my dreams did not want a pushover. He wanted a strong woman, as I wanted a strong man. I knew I would need a strong person to be my partner throughout life. However, I was not yet strong enough myself to attract my ideal partner to me. The Universe sent me experiences, painful ones, to help me grow into the woman I needed to be in order to have the man of my dreams.

After my first painful break-up, I beat myself up for the mistakes I believed I made. I took from that experience that I was a bad person. These feelings made me determined to prove what a good partner I could be in a relationship. The problem was that in trying to prove that I was good, I believed that I was not good. Hence, my thoughts of not being good attracted relationships in which I did not feel good enough for them. It was not until the pain associated with my failed engagement that I was able to see how these thoughts of not being good enough were neither true nor serving me.

By finally recognizing my truth from the pain I experienced, I owned the woman that I am. Once I did, it took three weeks and I attracted my soul-mate. I could not have the relationship that I do now with my husband if it were not for the past relationships that moved me to own the part of my womanhood and power that is my truth. In being in my truth, I attracted beyond what I thought was possible in a mate.

From Owning Our Power to Manifesting Our Desires

When experiences have not turned out in our favor, we ridicule ourselves, beat ourselves up, and abuse ourselves as to how we must have screwed something up. We may also blame others. What we certainly do not do is give thanks in those moments when the rug has been pulled out from underneath us. We are too upset, too hurt, and too much in pain. Of course, we need to allow ourselves to let these feelings out, because that is the truth about how we feel. Hence, I am *not* trying to have you pretend to be grateful or feel you should feel grateful when you do not. We must feel whatever we feel.

At some point, however, we will become tired of feeling upset. Usually we decide to put the experience behind us and move on with our life. If we truly want to move on rather than just put the experience behind us, we must allow to ask ourselves a critical question. Ask yourself the following: "Was I owning my truth, my magnificence, and my power?" If the answer is "no," great, because now we are one step closer to recognizing the abundance in all we are given.

In regard to my desire to get married, I first had to change my attitude about myself. My thoughts about myself in my early twenties were that I was not enough. I was not attractive, smart, or successful enough for someone to truly love me. After going through countless years virtually dateless and then finally getting engaged only to have it end, I finally had enough of buying into these lies! After crying my eyes out for two weeks straight, I realized my truth. My attitude changed from feeling worthless to owning the truth of who I am. Suddenly my internal dialogue switched from self-loathing beliefs to powerful thinking. My thoughts were, "If I am not enough for you then fine, but I am enough for me. I am enough. I am beyond enough and too bad for you that you cannot recognize it." Sure there was some anger in this statement, but that anger was good, as it touched into my power and allowed me to set my standard of never taking less than what I deserve in a relationship.

Even though I was still a bit stung after my engagement ended, I received the gift. This gift was one of my most treasured as I took back my power. I then gave thanks, because I knew I was becoming realigned again with my truth–that I was enough to have the love I dreamed of with my life partner. Through knowing my worth and giving thanks for the experiences that brought me to see clearly again, I was finally ready to attract exactly what I desired!

From all of our experiences, we are gaining strength in order that we have the ability to handle our heart's desires. We need to be grateful that the Universe is not giving us our desires just to have them taken away. The timing may not be right for us or for the other people involved. There is nothing wrong with this. It is an inner knowing that we are being molded in order to hold and accept the abundance we are to be given. If we do not believe in ourselves enough, we will not be able to handle these gifts. The Law of Attraction will not be in place. Like will not be with like and therefore cannot be.

The Joy of Not Having What We Desire

The joy of not having what I desire is a challenge for me to remember at times. I can be so focused on what I want to create and how amazing life will be when I create my heart's desire that I lose sight of the gifts in the present. After I receive what I have desired, then I am able to look back and say to myself, "Why was I so worried and anxious?" I realize I could have utilized the time when I was **in the process of receiving** so much better and had so much more fun if I was not worrying so much. **In the process of receiving** is how I now perceive the time when I have not yet fully achieved a desire of mine that I hold true and deep in my heart. Instead of thinking I do not have what I desire, and therefore I am coming from a place of lack, I believe and know that my desire is in the process of becoming a part of my life.

If I had had the belief that I was in the process of receiving in my previous experiences, I could have relaxed and enjoyed life more fully. I did not, though, because I lacked faith. Because my faith wavered at times, I would question and even persecute myself for not being able to manifest my dream. My fears would take over, sharing with me any and every shortcoming about myself that I could possibly have. I would buy into those fears because I took to heart other people's pain and fear that came through their words of discouragement. Being caught up in my old wounds and fears took me away from living my life consciously from my internal truth and in the present. I moved to focusing on my past and my pain when I lost faith in the present and the gifts available to me at that time.

To have faith means we are to be conscious and aware of all that is within us, knowing that it will provide for our every desire. When we are conscious, we know that we are not abandoned, because all that is happening is based on Divine Order. Through our trust in the Divine Order, our desires will occur beyond our imagination.

We want to believe that if we were just given our desire, all would be well for us. The movie *Bruce Almighty* starring Jim Carrey demonstrates very clearly that getting our desires does not take away all our problems. Even though he was given the powers of God to create any scenario he wanted, he could not impact matters of the heart that involve our free will. These must be addressed from within, and only we can do this.

We tend to think that we are all open and ready for our dream to come true. Yet most of us are not internally prepared to handle the magnificence we are asking for in our lives. We do not feel internally deserving enough, capable enough, or prepared enough to have our dream, and therefore we lose it. Instead, our experiences prepare us to be able to claim and cherish the desire that is within us. As part of our preparation, we go through experiences in which we *determine for ourselves* our strength, our power, our beauty, and our gifts. Without our ability to own these qualities, our desires would just slip out of our lives.

Thoughts Are Only the Beginning of Shaping Our Experiences

Our thoughts are an aspect of our creative energy. We have the ability to shape our thoughts and our perceptions. How we utilize this creative energy determines to what extent we are aligned with our truth. When our thoughts are not aligned with our truth, we can utilize our emotions to guide us back. Our emotions are connected to our experiences. Experiences are given to us to shape us and help us own our truth. When our thoughts and emotions are aligned with our truth, we are connected to our spiritual selves. From our spiritual selves, we have an inner knowingness that directs and provides us with all that we desire. From our Spirit is where abundance actually comes, as it is our tie to our Source. The more we are able to open ourselves to our truth and follow the guidance from within, the more easily we will be able to create the abundance we desire in every aspect of our life.

The Wizard of Oz is another great movie that demonstrates how our thoughts, emotions, and Spirit unite to manifest our desires. All the characters of the story already had within them the qualities or abilities they so deeply desired to have. They just could not recognize it yet because their thoughts were not aligned with the truth. After being given challenging experiences in which they had to address their fears, they were shown that they do have these qualities. All of the characters had to address their own fears in order to recognize within themselves that they had the abilities they desire. As they recognized the power within themselves, they became aligned with their inner knowingness, which allowed them to make life-altering changes. Again, these changes first had to begin with their internal processes in order to impact their lives.

Take the lion, for example. Courage did not mean attacking everyone at every opportunity, as he had first thought. That was his misperception of what courage meant. Until he was given the opportunity through his experiences, he could not find the true meaning of courage. Through being able to stand up for what he believed in and face adversity, he discovered the truth within himself. As he discovered the true meaning of his power, he was able to utilize his strength in a manner that was aligned with his true sense of self.

An Example of How We Unconsciously Block Creating Abundance in Our Lives

Recently I went to an event where one of the speakers was a woman sharing her story of living her dreams and encouraging others to do the same. Part of her story was how she had "paid her dues," meaning that she had gone through many jobs, failures, and time spent trying to reach her goal. When I heard her saying this, my Spirit started to cringe. The idea that we must "pay our dues" did not sit well with me. It is true that we may need to have certain experiences in order to own our truth. The crucial aspect is that we only need to "pay our dues" if we are unable to recognize our power.

Because most people do not know their power and all that they are capable of achieving, most people need to have experience after experience **to demonstrate to themselves** that they are capable. In trying to attain success, it may appear that we are trying to prove to others that we are talented. Really we are trying to prove our ego wrong about the self-imposed limitations we have bought into. We are learning to listen again to our inner voice, which knows the truth: that we are powerful beings.

By having experiences in which we listen to our gut and prove our ego wrong, we continue to demonstrate to ourselves that it is worth listening to our inner guidance. We learn we can trust our inner voice even if it is asking us to do things we never thought ourselves capable of achieving. This is all that we are doing when we are paying our dues: we are gathering up enough evidence for ourselves to see our magnificence in order that we can believe it for ourselves. Instead of being so hard on ourselves, we need to build on each small success that we make. The quicker we are able to honor our success, the easier it will be for us to take bigger risks. In the process, we reiterate to ourselves the truth of our ability to succeed and create all that we desire.

When the speaker at this event was able to acknowledge her abilities, she said she was able to "burst her own bubble." She recognized that she put her own invisible block around what she felt she was capable of achieving. It was not until she was ready to believe in herself enough that she could step into her dream life. She burst that bubble, meaning she was at a place where she was willing to own her truth. In hindsight, she also was able to realize that she was the only one who could recognize her abilities and decide to take ownership of all her magnificence. Regardless of what others told her about her abilities, how much she was paid, or what rewards she received, no one else could show her worth to her. Once she owned her worth and felt deserving of receiving, the opportunities became available to her to manifest her dreams. Nevertheless, because her experience was that she had to go through many trials and tribulations, she believes that this is the process to creating success.

The truth is that we can determine how long we need to drag out knowing our truth. We do not need endless experiences to recognize all the talents we have to offer the world. *The concept of "needing to pay our dues" can be a way to rationalize why we have not gotten what we desired in the time frame we expected.* It is a sense that we **had** to go through all those experiences. Sometimes we do in order to gain certain skills, this is true. Yet other times we only have to go through so much in order to prove to ourselves that we are worthy of all that we desire. We must understand that we do not have to put ourselves through the ringer in order to finally realize that we are talented human beings with gifts to offer the world.

A few people know their truth without question or without being concerned about what other people think. They listen to their gut and follow it without hesitation and without needing the approval of others. Because of this, they will often experience what society considers success at a young age. I believe we are going to see this more often, as more children are being born without the need to go through the process of remembering their truth. It is as if these souls have been here enough times to know how silly it is not to know their truth. Thus, they decide to know their magnificence and follow their intuition at all times. In doing so, they model to us how easily we can create what we desire in life if we decide to know our truth as well.

Many people do not want to view life as easy, because then it makes them feel like they did something wrong, since their life did not feel easy to them. This is why notions that "there is no easy ride, we must pay our dues, and life is hard" penetrate our culture so deeply. It is as if the theme song for so many is "It's a Hard Knock Life" from the musical *Annie*. It is important to understand, though, that if we feel that we are going to get knocked around by life, then we will.

Remember, we must only need to respond to the best of ability in being responsible toward our life. We are not meant to be perfect or else we could not continue to grow and create the joyful life we desire. We are not required to know any more than we do when we are responding the best we know how to in that present moment. The bottom line in our experiences is that we can choose to buy into what a "screwup" we are when our life does not go as planned and put ourselves through endless experiences in order to finally get that we are not lacking in any way. The other choice is to see the gift in our experiences—what we can learn from them to create what we desire—while still believing that we are on our way to manifesting our dream life.

We Need to Know that We Are Deserving of Abundance to Receive Abundance

A phrase that I often use and like is, "God does not give us more than we can handle." Most often this phrase is utilized to state that our Creator will not give us any experience that is insurmountable for us. The phrase emphasizes that we will always be cared for and supported, especially when we feel challenged. I think this phrase is also pertinent to describing our ability to handle good experiences as well. In being able to handle the gifts that God intends for us, we must feel deserving and worthy of all the abundance the Universe gives us in the present. Unfortunately, too many of us do not recognize our experiences as gifts that allow us to prepare for being able to handle the good that is intended for us.

Allow me to explain how we do not receive abundance in our lives. I see many people, including myself at times, who are so willing to blow off a simple thank-you. It is as if we somehow do not even feel deserving of any gratitude. Our response is to discount ourselves, stating something like, "It was nothing." Even though it felt effortless on our behalf, our actions do not equate to nothing. What we did was obviously important, because our actions impacted another person enough to be thankful for our efforts.

The truth is that when we are living in our truth and creating from our Spirit, it will feel easy and effortless. This is how we are supposed to manifest abundance. Yet when we act based on being moved by our Spirit without a second thought and equate that to "nothing," we are missing the gift. By dismissing the gift of our inner guidance, we are disabling ourselves from accepting the abundance the Universe desires us to have through simply living through our Spirit. We are given the experience of a compliment to enjoy the satisfaction of being in Spirit and to continue to fuel us to remain living that way.

By being willing to receive a compliment, we are taking in how good it feels to live through our Spirit and how easy it is to manifest abundance in our lives. When we accept a compliment, it feels good. Notice, however, that when we cannot take in a compliment, we do not feel as good internally. We do not feel that good because we were given a gift and declined. We must ask ourselves if we are not willing to accept a compliment, how on earth will we be able to accept the gifts that our souls long for us to have?

When We Live from Our Spirit, Nothing Is "Too Good To Be True."

When we hand over our life to trusting our Spirit to guide us and believe in our power to create abundance, we will be shocked by how easy it is to manifest. In fact, we will likely try to dismiss the gifts we are being given. Because we lacked the struggle in obtaining what we desired, we will feel like there is something wrong with what has been brought into our lives. Unfortunately, the only problem will be our perception that life cannot be this easy. The truth is, it can.

I am speaking from my own experience when I first began manifesting my desires. The little surprises, I was okay with and accepted with ease. Getting the table I desired at a restaurant, finding the closest parking space, or spotting money that was left right under my feet when no one else was around was a lot of fun to receive. However, when I started to manifest in areas in my life that really mattered to me, I got scared.

At the time, I did not realize that I was scared. As I look back, I realize how getting what I desired really threw me for a loop. I was in disbelief because *I was caught up in the misconception that I need to do something to earn what I desire*. My mind comprehended that in being aligned with our Source, I would automatically attract that which I desire. Emotionally, however, I became all bent out of shape and was questioning the gifts I received when they would just fall into my lap. It took some time for my body, mind, and Spirit to adjust to accepting the abundance I was being given. In the following examples, I will demonstrate how we can contort what we are given, even when we are receiving what we desire.

My Challenge with Accepting God's Abundance

When I first began claiming my power, I felt so good inside. I felt like I was walking on cloud nine as the world became open for me to experience all that I desired. Possibly for the first time ever in my life, I saw what I was capable of creating, and I was enjoying living life.

Feeling as good as I did, I was ready to finally put out to the Universe what I truly desired. I made a list of what I would like to accomplish with my career. I wanted to have three new clients within three months. Within days, I had two new clients, and it completely freaked me out! I was in disbelief because at the time I was not even trying.

What had happened was that I was taking a two-day spa getaway with my best friend. The next thing I knew, I met someone at the restaurant the first night of our trip and I had a client. The following day, I was getting a pedicure and had another client. Of course, I was thrilled! A part of me, however, also became scared. All of a sudden I questioned if this was really what I wanted and if I could handle all of this responsibility. After those two clients, I did not receive a new client for almost six months.

Another example occurred this past summer, when I was feeling challenged with finding permanent, part-time care for my children. Because I needed help just twice a week, it seemed the only people who could help me out were college students. When I hired them, I had to contend with their schedules during the day and their leaving for extended periods of time when they were on break. Neither of those scenarios was my ideal. With precision, I visualized what I desired and found exactly what I was looking for in a sitter. She was perfect for our needs and took to the job effortlessly. Three weeks later, I got news that she was being deported back to India.

As I look back on these experiences, I can see that I was unable to accept the abundance that I was being given. I doubted these gifts. When I received clients, I doubted my ability to be able to manage working while also raising my children. In regards to my sitter, my underlying thoughts were that she was too good to be true. Therefore, what happened in each case? My sitter was gone and no more clients appeared. I was given gifts, gifts that I prayed for over and over to occur. Then I doubted the gifts when they appeared. Instead of being full of gratitude, I began looking for what was wrong with what I received.

In both examples, I came to realize that I was fearful when I received what I desired. When I doubt the gifts I have received, how could they possibly stay in my life? Then it hit me that my thoughts really are this powerful! This is scary to me, because then I have to be so intricately **aware** of what it is going through my mind and address my fears, doubts, and old tapes that limit me by believing "we can't have it all."

We have all heard the saying that God is willing to give to those who are willing to receive. I always thought of myself as a person who is willing to receive. At that point, however, I had to question whether I truly am willing. Am I really? I have to look at all I am asking from God, the big and the small, and question this now. The Universe gives me gifts, ones that are very important to me, yet when I receive those that were not even my "big ones," I dismiss them as impossible. If I do this with a babysitter or a couple of new clients, how on earth am I going to be able to receive my greater desires if they were ever to occur? It is like being handed a gift and handing it right back because it is too perfect. What am I saying to myself? Am I saying, "No thanks, that was too easy. I don't deserve that?"

The tricky part is that at that time I did feel deserving, which is why I was able to attract those experiences in my life. It was my underlying perceptions about abundance that needed to be addressed. The important question for me became, "How do I change the thoughts and beliefs about abundance that have been ingrained in my mind?" It is through the process of being conscious of my thoughts and doubts to discover the underlying message that I am supposed to learn. This message–to always check in with my truth–tells me to have true and unwavering faith in the abundance that is within me.

The phrase, "Ye of little faith," plays over and over in my mind when I am not trusting in the Universe's ability to provide for me. Our society teaches us to question, doubt, and scrutinize to a fault. We are taught the opposite of living in faith as we learn to allow our inaccurate perceptions to rule our thoughts. What can be difficult to recognize is how much these thoughts are truly impacting our lives. The only way to acknowledge these thoughts that do not serve us is to look at when something that we desired does not turn out as we expected. As we already know, nothing actually "goes wrong," since every experience is an opportunity to learn and grow in order that we may manifest our heart's desires.

When we do not experience all that we desire, it is imperative at this point to examine what thoughts we had about our experience while it was occurring. Recognize both the supportive and the non-supportive thoughts, ideas, and beliefs regarding the situation. We must realize that our misperceptions had overpowered any positive outlook that we may have had. In order to stop the same outcome from continuing in the future, we must address those misperceptions that did not support us toward being aligned with what our heart desires. Demonstrating to our minds that those non-supportive thoughts are not true is crucial. We can prove to our rational minds that our thoughts are false by giving evidence of the opposite. We need to remind ourselves of examples in which we were living in our truth, power, and magnificence.

In my case with the sitter, the non-supportive thoughts I had were, "This is too easy. There must be something wrong with her." If I do this with my sitter, look at all the other opportunities and gifts I must simply pass up because I believe "this is too good to be true." We are taught in opposition to God's truth. How many times have we heard, "If is seems too good to be true, it is?" So we become programmed to dismiss, question, and doubt to the point that we get scared when we receive. When we are in fear, we cannot hear our instincts. We have replaced our inner knowing with the belief that it is difficult to receive all that we desire. If this is our belief, our desires will not come to us so easily. Therefore, we tend to receive with challenge and suffering rather than with grace and ease.

I had to sit down and help myself remember that having excellent support and a career that allows me to express my passion are exactly what I am meant to have. Can I accept it?

If I can, it will come easily and it will be perfect. THIS IS HOW THE DIVINE WORKS, GIVING US EXACTLY WHAT IS PERFECT FOR US!!! "Do not doubt this truth, my love," is the voice I hear within as the Divine yearns for me to be able to accept all that the Universe wants me to receive. I then challenged those programmed thoughts about how life is hard and proved to my rational mind that those thoughts are indeed false.

Some of my best and most significant choices were made spur of the moment. When I looked at those moments when I did not question my gut and the gifts I was receiving, I saw how easily those gifts manifested in my life. In those moments, I was open to receiving and allowing into my life the abundance that is within me to come out and be present in my life.

The Universe gives all of us experiences in which we are easily open to receiving as well as situations in which we reject abundance in order that we may recognize how powerful we truly are. We came to learn experientially by seeing that through our thoughts, we can equally create a miserable, dramatic, or challenging life **as easily** as we can create a beautiful life! If we do not think this statement is true, this is where our work begins, for this is how we are not open to receiving.

Surrendering to All of the Abundance We Are Given

Of course, if we can recognize that we struggle with accepting the gifts that we do want, we can really feel challenged to accept the abundance that we did not ask to come into our lives. Some of the gifts we receive do not always feel like gifts at the time because they test us. Many of us recognize that our greatest opportunities often appear as obstacles. My only relief then is to surrender my will to God's will and trust in the infinite wisdom of the Universe.

This brings to mind when I found out I was pregnant with my twin boys. The morning of my first ultrasound with them

I meditated as usual and was told "I will not be given any-thing I cannot handle." I was therefore a bit apprehensive about this ultrasound. To my astonishment and complete surprise, I was pregnant with twin boys. I was shocked and scared. After all, the age between the boys and my oldest daughter would only be twenty months. (They were preemies and ended up being only eighteen months apart!)

My husband and I were excited by the news of twins, but my fear about having twins was overwhelming to me. Instead of hiding my fear, I allowed my feelings to come through me as I cried for three days straight. I questioned how I would handle three young babies. Then peace came over me, and I knew that I would be fine. In fact, I felt so incredibly blessed to have two children come into my life through one preg-nancy. I knew it would be extremely special to be a part of the lives of two souls who decided to enter this life together. Nevertheless, I still had some fears about having twins. The difference was that my fears no longer had control, as I was able to recognize the gift.

In order to help me work through my fears, the Universe presented me with opportunities to buy into my fears or choose differently. While I was pregnant, every encounter I had with a mother of twins was filled with horror stories about how difficult it has been for her raising twins. I simply told myself that would not be my experience. As it has turned out, it has not been. My children have given me challenges, but they have also allowed me to grow. Without their pres-ence, I would not have been able to demonstrate to myself how capable I am in such a concrete manner. I would also not have known how to ask and accept the support my soul desired. All of my children are truly a gift for reasons that cannot be expressed in words!

The pattern again is simple: our thoughts, emotions, and inner knowing create abundance. When my thoughts went to my fears instead of my truth, I was given experiences to support me to choose thoughts that will serve me. I could determine through my experiences how I felt. I recognized that I did not feel good when I bought into the fear. I felt empowered, however, when I chose to create my own story regarding how my life would be with twins. I had experience after experience to gain an inner knowingness within myself, to see which path felt better and more aligned with my desires. As my thoughts, emotions, and inner wisdom connected, I experienced the abundance I was meant to receive.

By learning how to become capable, willing, and receptive to every form of abundance, we will give thanks for all of the gifts that come into our lives. We are able to claim this for ourselves whenever our thoughts are not aligned with our truth. We can see the pattern that will authentically allow us to find our truth again, which is beyond positive thinking. We can give ourselves experiences that are aligned with the feeling state of that which we desire. As we feel what we desire, our thoughts will automatically begin to shift back to our truth. Through becoming realigned with our truth, we are connecting to the internal abundance within ourselves. In being able to claim the abundance within ourselves, we will be able to recognize the power that is within each of us to create the life we want to have. This abundance is within us all, waiting to be recognized and freed to be expressed in the world. Our only job is to open ourselves to connect with our inner source in order that the abundance we desire flows through us and into our lives.

I dedicate this chapter to my boys, Jonah and Elijah, as I write about them on their second birthday. Happy Birthday boys! Thank you, thank you, thank you for deciding to be a part of my life this go-around. I am extremely blessed to be around such beautiful souls who deepen my learning and growth. I love you both!

Putting this Chapter into Practice:

1) Examine your life and write down all that you have created regardless of how you judge your manifestations. Can you find a sense of gratitude for all that you have created? Allow what you have manifested to serve you to gain even further clarity as to what your soul longs for and ask for assistance with being able to receive this gift. For instance, even if you feel that you have a rocky marriage, a part of you desired to get married and you manifested that in your life. Allow yourself to find gratitude for the experiences with your partner that brought you joy, while also defining what more your soul is longing for in your marriage. This may mean that you are grateful for the sense of humor that brought you and your mate together and you long for more tenderness between one another. Without placing blame, you are making your desires more clear, which allows the Universe to work through you.

2) Whatever statements or thoughts you use often in regard to money, check in with yourself and determine not only whether they are true but do they serve your highest good. For instance, instead of saying, "I cannot afford this," share your real truth. The real truth that will support you to continue to perceive abundance is, "I am not willing to spend my money on this currently." By being conscious of the words you choose, you eliminate buying into a sense of lack by owning your power of choice for how you would like to utilize your energy resources.

3) Create an abundance board to support you to visualize all that you desire to create. In the center of the board should be a picture of you. Around your image, create or cut out symbolic pictures of the emotional experiences you desire to feel more frequently. Perhaps you desire to feel more joy, passion, spiritual connection,

or power. These images could be anything as long as when you see them, they remind you of the emotional state you desire. For instance, joy may be of a person laughing while powerful may be a picture of a mountain. Around the outside of the emotional abundance you desire to create is where you can place the physical desires you want to manifest such as money, a boat, or trips to the spa. As you attend to your internal well-being, watch how the external experiences begin to manifest. Your board becomes your proof that visually demonstrates that when you authentically address your internal needs, you are able to create your ideal life.

Chapter 10
Letting Go of Our Expectations in Order to Attain Our Desires

A s we are now at a point at which we are able to see that we have the power to manifest our dreams, we will face our final challenge, which is letting go. Ultimately we do not have a say whether what we desire will or will not occur in our lives. For this reason, an important part about learning to manifest is letting go of what it is we desire. We do our part to create, visualize, and put forth all of the energy within ourselves to manifest our desire. Once we do our part, which includes all those aspects previously covered in this book, we need to let go.

Although it may feel like we are letting go of our dream, in reality, we are only letting go of our expectation of what the outcome of our efforts should look like to us. Many spiritual writings have suggested not having expectations in order to prevent us from being hurt when life does not go according to our plans. After all, it is our expectations and not life that causes us pain. Nevertheless, most of us still have expectations. This chapter will discuss how we can support ourselves with being able to let go, which will allow us to better manage our expectations.

Finding Peace Even When Our Expectations Are Not Met

For whatever reasons, I have not relinquished having expectations. Expectations are still a part of my life, and I notice their existence when I am in pain because some experience did not turn out in a way that I desired. In the past, not having my expectations met could really throw me for a loop. Depending on how much I cared about an experience happening, I could be impacted for days, months, even years. I am not kidding when I say years, as it took me three years to completely get over the end of my first real relationship.

Today not having my expectations met still causes me to feel angry, frustrated, and sad in the short term. However, in the long run, my faith is deepened. Why would my faith deepen when I do not get what I desire? Because after I stop complaining to the Universe and everyone around me, I trust that I am still being taken care of for my highest good. Having this faith gives me a sense of peace when I cannot rationally figure out the reason why my life did not go according to plan. As I peacefully go about living again, the answers quickly come to me.

Finding my sense of peace is what allows me to realign with Spirit in order that I can be open to the Universe and the gifts being offered. I am able to find peace again when I humbly remind myself that indeed the Universe is wiser than I am. The Universe takes care of my long-term well-being and is willing to sacrifice my short-term expectations. In order to be able to achieve all that my soul truly desires, not having all of my short-term desires may be something that needs to occur. I am not always so willing to forgo the short-term pleasures as much. Therefore, the Universe needs to help me out to stay on track for what is ultimately best for me.

My Expectation of How I Should Receive Inspiration

A simple example of an expectation I had not too long ago was when my family and I decided to go up to our condo in Door County, a popular vacation destination in northeastern Wisconsin. It was the beginning of fall, and I was very much looking forward to seeing the beauty of the changing leaves. I am so taken with trees that I wanted to spend the following two weekends up there as well. "After all," I thought, "these trees provide me with inspiration, and what is better than that?" Of course, there was a voice inside me saying that I should stay home and take care of some neglected areas around the house. Nevertheless, I convinced myself that I could get all my chores done if we got back at a reasonable time on Sunday.

That Friday evening we packed up the kids and went, even though my husband was not fond of going this particular weekend. (Normally he is chomping at the bit to go, but this weekend he felt there was too much he wanted to get done at home). We got there and our kids would not sleep, so we ended up getting one of the worst night's sleep in a long time. We woke up and had a challenging morning as well. Our dog ended up urinating and vomiting in the living room, while the kids were extraordinarily cranky from their lack of sleep the night before. Further, they did not nap that afternoon. To top things off, my husband and I got in a spat.

Because of my need to see the fall colors and be inspired, I wanted to try to stick it out and not go home. I compromised with my husband that if the kids did not go to bed that evening, we would leave. Sure enough, both my twin boys figured out how to jump out of their pack-n-plays for the first time, refusing to go to sleep. I gave in and packed us up.

Needless to say, I was not happy. Because I have now gotten used to manifesting in my life, my desires typically occur despite the odds. I was actually in shock and disbelief at what a trying weekend it became. My desire was to get away and enjoy the beauty with my husband and kids. "Why would the Universe not want me to experience this?" I thought. "Seeing the fall colors is fuel for my soul. Why would the Universe not support that?" I questioned. I was sad at the thought of not feeling supported. I was also extremely frustrated with my children. The weekend felt like such a bust and completely the opposite of what I desired.

I drove the three-hour trip home that night, which allowed me time to think. First, I had to vent all my frustration. I was gasping in tears at the thought of not being supported. The thought of not being able to return to our condo with my kids, since they would not sleep there, also made me extremely upset. I felt like the victim. "How could God do this to me?" I knew it was not the end of the world, but it was important to me.

After ten minutes of crying, I knew I had to search for peace. I prayed. In fact, I recalled a portion of a book I was reading by Sonia Choquette called *Trust Your Guides*. In her book, she tells us how to call on the archangels for assistance. I did just that, and in doing so, I began to find peace. Deep within me I knew there must be some reason I was supposed to be back home. I hoped it was not an emergency, but I trusted that I was very much supposed to be in our home the next day. Having trust and faith in the Universe's wisdom, I let go of the last twenty-four hours and began looking forward to a Sunday at home with my family. I also prayed for sleep!

After a great night's rest and all the kids sleeping in, we woke up very refreshed. I then remembered that there was a marathon going right past our home. I put on some sweats and dragged my kids outside with me in their pajamas to see the runners who just began to come by our home.

I was taken by these runners who had worked so hard to get to this day, thinking about how many of them, at one point in their life, probably could never even have comprehended the notion of running a marathon–and here they were. Then I saw a couple of families who were following a loved one in order to offer support. I was filled with tears. I did not know any of the participants in this race, yet I was filled with tears for them. I was witnessing them fulfilling a dream!

As a witness, I became *extremely inspired*. I began telling the runners how inspiring they were to me as they ran or walked by, and I felt I had a purpose being there. How beautiful was this moment, I thought, created with force on God's part to make me be there. I was filled with so much love and energy from seeing those runners take action toward their dreams, and I was so happy to be able to admire their hard work! Then it hit me. This is why I was meant to be home. God wanted me to be inspired by these runners. I was filled with gratitude for how the Universe will work so hard, often through my precious children, in order to get me to be where I am supposed to be in life.

I have seen the wonders and workings of the Universe in such greatness throughout my life. I am so grateful that I am at a place of peace, inspiration, and love after being lost for so long. I know that if our Creator can work through me, we all have hope.

Looking back, I can see how the Universe conspired to create all the events in my life, good and bad, in order for me to begin to know my truth. Now that I trust that the Universe takes care of me, I am on the lookout for the gifts when life does not go according to my plan. In doing so, I am not in a battle with the Divine. I no longer create suffering in my life by banging my head against the wall and asking "Why?" Okay, I still ask why when I fall into an old pattern of feeling like a victim, but thankfully it does not last very long. This is because I know that asking why is pointless. How can I ask why to God's infinite wisdom? It is as if I am saying my understanding surpasses the wisdom of the Universe.

I recognize that events happen to us that are so catastrophic that we are melted to our core and in unfathomable pain. In those cases, we are likely going to ask why, and that will be part of our healing process. In those times, all we can do is listen to our feelings and work through them. Our feelings heal us if we allow ourselves to be present with them.

Notice in my simple example of being disappointed how I still allowed my feelings to come through me as I was driving home. Even though mentally I could have talked myself out of expressing my thoughts and feelings about being disappointed because it was not a catastrophic event, I did not do that. I chose to express my emotions because I know it is cathartic to be in my truth, whatever my truth may be at that moment. In doing so, I released my pain and let go of being the victim in order that I could begin to find my way to peace again. Once I found peace, I was led to how I was supposed to experience inspiration, which of course went beyond my expectations!

Ensuring Our Way to Peace

If we have such a stranglehold on our lives and all that we expect to have happen to us, we certainly are not being open to the wisdom of the Universe. From my experience and those of my clients, I recognize how we can easily fall into having tunnel vision as to the manner in which our dreams should unfold. In fact, when we begin to recognize our power in being able to manifest our desires, it can feel even more crushing when something does not occur according to our vision. After all, we did our internal work and followed our inner guidance, yet our desire did not happen. What went wrong? We did not let go!

Sometimes we may be so determined to make our dream occur, we will be damned if it does not. We exhaust ourselves trying to put a square peg in a round hole. It does not work, yet we try over and over again, getting the same unsatisfactory results. In those moments when we feel we are banging our heads against a wall, the only option we have not tried is surrendering to what is our reality. Yet we are too afraid to surrender because we fear that would mean we are giving up on our dream. We are also afraid of the lack of meaning our life will have if our dream does not happen. We are counting on our dream to fulfill us in some way, and without our dream, we would feel hopeless about our life. "What would be the point of existence?" we question.

By surrendering to our fears of not accomplishing our dream, we allow ourselves to feel whatever it is we are feeling about our life. Again, if we are willing to be guided, our emotions will be the key. Although it may feel dismal to feel hopeless about our dream, we must surrender. Our fear is that if we surrender, we must give up on our dream. In fact, we only need to give up on *how* we feel we *should* attain our dream or what attaining our dream *should* look like.

The truth is, we feel hopelessness for a reason. When we feel hopelessness, this means we should no longer be going about living in the manner that we have been. How we are living currently is hopeless, which means we need to make a change. Many times this involves being willing to give up on the life that we planned in order to open ourselves to the one the Universe intends for our soul to experience. Of course, I recognize that giving up and letting go is much easier said than done. Nevertheless, we need to resolve ourselves to the fact that we do not have many other choices.

Choice number one is to be a victim and be mad at our Creator or whomever else we can blame that our dream has not occurred. Choice number two is to not give up while feeling exhausted and frustrated by our efforts, which still do not manifest our dream. Choice number three is to be willing to listen to our inner guidance even when it is telling us something that we do not want to hear. Choice one leaves us depressed and angry, choice two leaves us spinning our wheels while still feeling angry, and choice three can bring us peace. The bottom line is that if we cannot have the desire as we imagined it, we still need to go on living. How we go about our living is up to us. We can choose to have trust in the Universe that our desires will be provided for, or not.

Please do not get me wrong, as I know how scary this all sounds. It sounds incredibly scary to me as I write these words in a book that is very much a part of my dream to be able to write for a living. I will put my heart and soul into making this dream occur. Yet if my dream does not happen, I trust enough in the Universe's wisdom to guide me through my journey. Of course, if my dream does not occur as I would have liked, I will be disheartened. Another part of me knows that I am still better off for having tried. I challenged myself and accomplished something that I never imagined myself capable of doing. Furthermore, I trust that ultimately the feelings that I desire to experience will still happen, even if it is not in the manner in which I thought they would occur.

At one point when I was writing this book, I felt that if my dream did not occur, I would feel ruined. As I felt those emotions pouring out of me, even before I had a chance to finish this book, I was brought to remember my truth. If I use this book as proof that I am wise, good at my work, or somehow a better person, I know I will be crushed. On the other hand, if I write this book to guide, express, challenge, and remind myself of my truth, then I have accomplished my goal.

The truth is that this book is for me. If my experiences and the words I have written can support others as they have for me to understand my emotions and live more in my truth, then I am further blessed. If not, I have still been immensely blessed because I have honored this process of creating. Having the process of challenging myself and addressing my fears to write and express myself freely has filled my life with great passion. The energy shifted for me when I did not put so much weight on the outcome of this book as a reflection of me. Knowing that my worth will not change to any more or any less within me regardless of the outcome of this book has freed me. I am free to live in my truth and know my worth just being who I am and allowing myself to be guided throughout life.

As I came from feeling defined by this book to remembering my truth, I was able to let go of my need for external validation. This is what I wrote:

> The truth is that with or without this book I am wise, I am good at what I do, and I am worthy. It does not matter how many clients' lives I have changed or how many books I do or do not publish–I am worthy. I am worthy and wise because I have changed my life. I am worthy and wise because I make changes occur that are

aligned with my ideal. I am worthy and wise because I live a life from love. I am worthy and wise because I care. I am worthy and wise because I have made so many changes. I have put so much time and energy toward creating a life that feels good to me, a life in which I now feel good living in my body. I am worthy and wise because I feel much more at peace. I am worthy and wise because I have worked toward living my life being connected to my Source and coming to honor and respect the guidance and gifts I receive.

When I was able to recognize that there is nothing outside myself that can prove how good I am at helping people live their best life, I was able to let go. I can only help myself live my best life, and in doing so, I feel good. Ultimately feeling purposeful, passionate, abundant, and full of life is my goal. Trusting that this will occur is all I need to know within myself, as I create change and live from my heart.

What had switched for me inside was recognizing that I was already living my dream. When I looked at my dream in my twenties, it was to have a loving husband and family, to feel at peace within, and to feel a love for life. As my dream expands, I feel open to the possibilities offered by the Universe. I offer seeds of hope toward my desires, yet I let go of those seeds that are supposed to take hold and flourish and those that are not. Being able to let go has occurred through knowing that my dreams will manifest, even though it may not happen when and how I thought they should.

Regaining Focus toward Our Internal Process Is Crucial to Manifesting

If the only option for the Universe is to manifest our desires according to *our* plan, we are losing our internal focus. We are becoming overly focused on what the outcome should look like, when it should occur, and how happy we will be when our desire happens rather than remembering to be present with our internal process. Focusing on the external is how we lose our sense of peace. With our focus on the external, we become overly focused on the outcome that we desire, which makes us have blinders on to the rest of life that is going on around us. If we are doing this, we have lost the point, as we are no longer truly living. We cannot feel as if we are freely living when we are tied to the external.

Living freely does not mean we cannot dream about what we desire. We should dream; however, we need to trust in the flow of the abundant stream that is taking us to our desired experiences. When we are focused internally, we are as much enjoying the journey in creating what we desire as we are excited for the outcome to occur. We can only experience joy in the creation process if we can let go of the outcome and trust that it will occur at the time that is perfect for us.

One common way in which I, in the past, and many other people that I know have lost their joy is toward their journey with dating. Many of us get to a point in which we recognize that we desire to marry and then get extremely anxious about whether the relationship will result in marriage. The relationship can be going about wonderfully, yet when we hit our fear about marriage, we panic. Our anxiety can create upheaval in an otherwise solid relationship because we become overly focused on the external. Through our fear and anxiety, we continue to distance ourselves so far from our truth that it is impossible for us to connect with our soul-mate. We cannot connect with another if we are disconnected from ourselves.

If we let go and continue to have faith, we will find the beauty in all the aspects of our journey. We must remember that the process of whatever we are creating is unique with each different component of our life that we manifest. If we are not present in the process of our creation, we miss the joy, beauty, and love of what we are creating. For instance, we only get that early love phase once in each relationship, or experience a child's infancy one time, or feel the excitement and passion when we are creating something that is pertinent to our lives in that moment. Even though we may have each of these experiences more than once, we only get one shot to enjoy each particular creation we manifest. If we miss out on our first child's infancy, we will not be able to make that up with a second child. For that first child, it was a missed opportunity to enjoy that part of the journey. This does not mean that all is lost. Hopefully, however, these experiences help us to remember to enjoy what we have in the present rather than becoming overly focused on what we desire to have in the future.

In order that we do not miss out on further manifestations, we are reminded to slow down and enjoy the evolutionary process as we bring into reality what our hearts long to experience. When we are focused purely on the outcome, we risk needing to go through the experience again even after we obtained our desire. This may occur because we did not obtain all the gifts from the experience that we were meant to have. There is so much pleasure to be had throughout the process of creating if we can let go of needing a guarantee that our efforts will turn out exactly as we desire.

Letting Go of Our Dream Can Actually Open Us to Receive More

Remember that letting go of our expectations is different than letting go of our dreams. We can let go of what we expected or wanted to have occur in our life while still trusting that God will provide us with the type of experience that we wanted to have. If we look past the rigidly focused notion of our dream, there is a deeper emotional experience that can take shape in a multitude of forms. Sometimes our version of the dream could be too narrow for all that God intends for us. We must trust that God knows what is in our hearts and that will happen. We need to be willing to let go of our limited version of that experience, however, in order to have the abundance that the Universe desires to give each of us.

For myself, this occurred with me needing to let go of thinking I should have more clients. I thought if I wanted to be a success, more clients would be a necessary part of this equation. Of course, I was frustrated and upset when opportunities would not turn out and I would question my abilities. When I was able to honor the fact that, for whatever reason, I was not to have clients at this time, I found peace. In order to be at peace, I had to confront how I was using the number of clients I had to prove my worth to myself. Once I faced that I wanted to use the external to prove my worth, I was able to let go.

Timing Is Everything

At first, I could not understand why I was not getting the number of clients I desired. I felt like I was on the right path, so why not send clients my way, I wondered. I then allowed myself to sit still and listen. I accepted the fact that at this time, I was not supposed to have any more new clients. It did not mean that I was not good enough yet at the services I provided. In fact, the message I got was, "Your children need you right now. You are needed to create a solid foundation of love and limits that will carry your family forward." Again, no booming voice, just a message I heard in my head.

As it turns out, not having any new clients had a two-fold purpose. Knowing that I was supposed to be with my kids while they were young allowed me to really sink into the role of stay-at-home mom. Being at home with them was a gift for me and my kids. I looked at my experience in a new light. If I were to write the script for my life, it would be that I would be able to be with them while they were young. Therefore, I am having my dream come true. As long as I was able to trust that the other part of my desire involving my career would occur even though there was no proof of it in the present moment, I would feel at peace. Not only did I feel at peace, I felt like I was finally a part of the Universal flow, as I learned to accept rather than fight what my reality was at the time.

The other piece to me not having any new clients was that it turned me on to writing. If I had had more clients, I would not have had the yearning to express myself. Even more important is the fact that I would not have had the time for both my writing and my family. Prior to this experience, I would have never considered myself a writer. Now writing feels so right to me, as I am filled with passion about being able to express myself in this manner. Every time I am guided to write, I feel incredibly blessed.

The Further We Are Willing to Go, the Further We Will Be Taken

As we learn to let go of our expectations, we recognize that we begin to find peace as we surrender to the journey that the Universe is offering us. Oftentimes as we learn to trust the flow of the Universe, we will find that we are being asked to let go of more than just our life's plan. We are also being called to let go of notions of ourselves that are no longer our truth. In other words, the process of creating internal shifts is an ongoing process, regardless of how ideal our life is.

Because life is constantly changing us, we will desire to remain connected to our truth. In fact, we will likely find that the more we are able to manifest, the more we are being called to further own our truth. For this reason, we will be called to go deeper and address aspects of ourselves that no longer fit as our truth because of our greater connection to our essence. This calling is to allow us to connect more deeply to our Source, which will allow greater abundance to come forward through us.

For many of us, when we are being called to recognize more of our truth, it is because a part of us continues to identify aspects of ourselves from our past, whether good or bad. Other times we create notions of what our experiences should be like based on our observations of others. Neither of these notions is our true calling.

In order for us to claim who we are in the present and future, we must let go of who we once were if it is no longer our truth. As we age, we tend to want to hang onto aspects of ourselves from our youth. Whether that is looking young and svelte, being as skilled in a certain area that we once did well in, or expressing ourselves sexually in the same manner as we did earlier in our lives, these aspects of ourselves will likely change the more mature we become. We struggle with this change as we desperately try to keep who we are the same–when we are meant to be different. Maybe we are not as slender, but the gift is for us to have a greater sense of peace toward how we look. Letting go of the skill that we once had allows us to open a new chapter in our lives. Perhaps we feel less erotic because we have sex less often, yet we can appreciate the gift of a more intimate relationship with a lover over time.

Instead of constantly struggling to maintain the past, we are being called to let go and accept our present gift. If we continue to yearn for aspects of our youth, we will have a constant sense of lack in our present. This sense of lack, in turn, has us utilizing our energy for an aspect of ourselves that is meant to be a part of our past–we are not intended to regain it. Utilizing our energy in this manner becomes fruitless, and we become depleted.

On the other hand, when we are able to let go of the past, we free our energy to put toward our present desires, purposes, and passions. We grow and change, and as we do, what we desire will change with us. Seeing what we want to create and manifest is the fun of the journey. Where our souls take us is often so surprising that we are filled with bliss! To create bliss in our present, we cannot expect that the route that brought us joy will be the same route to our inner sense of happiness or contentment time and again. Just think about what you focused on as an adolescent and how much that has changed for you because your goals have changed based on your experiences.

If we are up for being surprised and filled with passion toward our lives, we must also be willing to let go of how most people go through living their life. As we begin to make the changes in our life that our souls want us to make for our highest good, we may mourn aspects of our old life. If we are used to gossiping with friends, we may feel at a loss at first about how to carry on a conversation with others. If we are used to having a glass of wine each night or around friends, we may feel uncomfortable going without. After all, it is easier in ways to be unconscious, as we simply go along with what the majority is doing. However, if we want an extraordinary life, we will be going about our life differently from what is considered the norm. Let's face it: how the majority of our world functions is not for their highest good. Therefore, we must be willing to stick out a bit and deviate from the masses in order to create the changes in our lives that will lead us to creating our dream.

We are always being guided to accept the present in order that we understand the new gifts we are being offered. When we are willing to surrender both our dream and ourselves by having faith in God, we have learned the process of letting go. Throughout this journey, we will find that the more we are willing to let go, the more we will find ourselves aligning with our ideal.

Letting Go of Our Expectation of What Extraordinary Living Looks Like

As we find ourselves creating our ideal life, we must let go of any expectations around having a perfect life. We must not confuse perfectionism with our ideal. The truth is that we will not have what we truly desire if our lives are perfect. Perfect lives means there is no room to make mistakes, to grow, or to be free, which is not truly living. Truly living means we get to enjoy the full experience of life.

When we come from our inner knowingness, we are able to recognize that it is through the ordinary aspects of life that we realize many of our dreams. Sure, our dreams involve those extraordinary moments when we accomplish creating a long-time desire. However, it is in our day-to-day living that we create the emotional abundance that makes those external goals meaningful.

For instance, one desire for me is to experience love, connection, and peace within my family. Do I always have this experience with them? Of course not! I have challenging moments with my children and husband at times as well. However, I recognize that it is through those challenging, human moments that I am truly connecting. Together we are finding our way, which brings us the intimacy that I desire to have. If I did not go through those challenging experiences, I would not feel as emotionally and spiritually connected to my family as I do.

Of course, family and friends love to tease me about passing out my business cards when I have one of those extraordinary days with one of my children and I feel like I am the worst mom ever! Recently I went to my daughter's preschool for a Mother's Day party. After we had to leave the last preschool party early because one of my sons screamed the whole time, I was really hoping I would be able to enjoy myself this year. As I was sitting with my daughter and one of my sons, I looked to make sure my other son was behaving on the other side of the room. Out of the corner of my eye, I saw dirt, rocks, and plants being thrown in the air. Although I thought my son was playing in the pretend kitchen, he had instead found a garden to excavate and throw all over the floor. I was completely mortified as I dragged my screaming son out of the classroom, covered with dirt, with my other kids crying that they did not want to leave. As I left, I saw in the other mothers' eyes the look of pity, as they were so glad that they were not me at that moment.

Even though I was completely frustrated by my son's behavior, I would not change the challenging moments I have in life. I have found that it is through these less-than-ideal moments that I find out more about who I am, which in turn allows me to further my alignment with my truth. If it was not for me continuing to learn from the ordinary or challenging moments in my life, I would be without purpose and passion. In other words, living through the ordinary, day-to day-dealings is how I create my ideal.

My ideal relationship with my son forms as we learn how to work through problems together. Through having an experience like the one I mentioned, I get to know him more and he gets to know me more, even though there are aspects of one another that we would rather not have to deal with. Yet these are true aspects of ourselves. He is mischievous and curious at times, and I am angry and frustrated at times. Still, we love each other, and that shines through as we make amends. He does not have to pretend to be any different, nor do I, and through that, our bond becomes as I had always hoped: being connected, loving, and secure.

As we continue to create our ideal life, we must remind ourselves that while aspects of our lives will feel magical, others will still feel ordinary. Yet it is our perception of the ordinary that will be different. We can let go of feeling that in order to have our dream, our life should look a certain way or go as planned. Our gift will be feeling as blessed, abundant, and present through the outcome of our challenges as we do through the manifestation of the dream. When we are able to recognize that all our life experiences give us true meaning, we will see every aspect of our life as our dream.

Our Full-Circle Process

Through remembering our truth, we find peace. Through living in peace, we hear our inner guidance. Through trusting in our inner guidance, we create the life we desire. From the beginning of this book, we learned that we need to be open to all aspects of ourselves, including our emotions, ego, and fears. Whenever we experience those aspects, they are a part of us. Some of the feelings, behaviors, and thoughts that we do not approve of will remain part of us. Yet those aspects of ourselves make us who we are.

Letting go means that we do not have to feel that we must always be completely aligned with the Universe, in balance, or at peace. We must know within ourselves that we do not have to be perfect to manifest our dreams. We must simply have the intention to live our best life. With that intention, we will continue to grow.

The truth is that even after reading this book, we are still going to wish we had approached a situation differently or utilized our wisdom better. Our desire is to have those experiences less often. Only we can measure whether this growth is taking place within ourselves. For instance, if we used to berate ourselves over every little encounter and now we only do that once a day, we are already living a better life. Our growth needs to be our focus rather than feeling that we should never beat ourselves up again. If our focus is on perfection, we set ourselves up to fail. When our intention is about creating the best life based on ourselves regardless of what others may think, we are on the right path to manifesting our desires.

By allowing ourselves to just be, we automatically let go of expectations of ourselves. Being proud of ourselves for who we are–whether or not we have showered or are perfectly coiffed, belly is sticking out or is sucked in, or feeling angry or happy in any given moment–will allow us the freedom to truly live. We must experience freedom within ourselves first in order to experience this sense of freedom in our reality.

As we continue on our journey, remember that we are blessed to feel everything. Being able to feel all aspects of our true selves–including our fears, the challenges with our ego, and the ebb and flow of our emotions–is the gift of truly living. When we are able to work with rather than against ourselves to create the life we are intended to live, we feel our power. We are intended to experience the gamut of our emotional selves in order that to recognize all the gifts we have been given.

We must remind ourselves that we came here to have a human experience. In order to enjoy our human experience, we must allow ourselves to live truly and freely. We will only experience the awe and wonder of life when we let go of trying to deny our feelings, fears, and ego. Living is accepting all these aspects of ourselves. When we do, we let go of fighting ourselves and take in the gifts that are given in each moment that we breathe.

Enjoy this experience. May it be filled with belly laughter, heartfelt tears, passionate love, desperate pain, and anything else that will support you to truly live. When we grant ourselves permission to have the human experience, we begin to live as we are intended to, which is fully, passionately, and present in each moment we are given. Create to your heart's content, and then we will know when it is our time to let go of this journey.

Letting go is honoring the flux of our emotional selves that allows us to continue to be all that we are meant to be in this lifetime. We are Spirits in the human world. We must remember to respect ourselves for choosing this experience in the form that we have. We have chosen to find peace within without escaping to the top of a mountain. We are frontiers in creating a path of peace in our everyday existence. The way to this peace is letting go of our expectations that we should be or feel any different than who we are. When we are able to go with the abundant flow of the Universe rather than swim upstream, we will feel at peace. Believing that we must climb a mountain to attain success is Old World thinking. Allowing ourselves to go with the natural flow of life and knowing that we will experience all we desire from life will bring us the gift of truly living and enjoying the life we have.

We all know that we have the ability and power to create peace when we are willing to listen to our truth. Regardless of how we may still feel challenged by owning all aspects of ourselves, our desire to do so will allow us to honor life. As we honor all that we are and have been given, we are opening ourselves to receive all that our hearts desire. Effortlessly and with ease, one by one our intentions will manifest. As we create our ideal life, our hearts will overflow with gratitude for being given the gift to live authentically, freely, and abundantly.

The Universe supports each of us through experience after experience to own our power, to feel and know our worth from within, and to acknowledge our beauty regardless of our circumstances. If we can attain this within ourselves, then we will feel capable of receiving all the gifts God offers us. There will be no question of worthiness when we know our inner truth as being one in the same as God. This is what our Creator desires for us all. We are being supported to reach the point where we can become capable to **receive the gifts that are beyond our expectations**! Through following our unique essence that guides us, we will create a life greater than we ever dreamed possible.

Putting this Chapter into Practice:

1) Play. In what part of your life do you take yourself too seriously? If we take our selves and life too seriously, there is no time to play. Be silly, awkward, and risky as you express yourself without needing substances to free you to live from that state. Authentically express your joy for being here and creating all that you have.

2) Have a great picture of yourself in which you are fully living life in the present moment framed and in a place that you can see it as soon as you rise. Choose

to allow yourself the experience of fully living each day that you are given as it was intended for your highest good to experience.

3) Find an example in which something that you desired occurred. Examine the details and see for yourself if your desire happened as your expectations thought it should have happened. Was the timing as you had wanted it, or was it "packaged" as you would have thought? As we remind ourselves that we do get what is for our highest good yet often on different terms, we will be able to free our energy of anxiety and worry. Utilize this example to remember to fully enjoy the flow of life offered to us in each moment!

Order Form

To order additional copies, fill out this form and send it along with your check or money order to:

Living Source, LLC.
740 N. Plankinton, Suite 310
Milwaukee, WI 53203

Cost per copy $14.95 plus $5.00 P&H.

Ship _____ copies of *Emotional Abundance: Become Empowered* to:

Name:_____

Address:_____

City/State/Zip:_____

___ Check for signed copy

Please tell us how you found out about this book.

___ Friend   ___ Internet
___ Book Store   ___ Radio
___ Newspaper   ___ Magazine
___ Other _____